Essays on Exclusion

Our Critical, Collective Journey

Toward Equity in Education

Phillip A. Boda (Editor)

ISBN 978-1-64504-019-4 (Hardback)
ISBN 978-1-64504-018-7 (Paperback)
ISBN 978-1-64504-020-0 (E-Book)

Printed on acid-free paper

© DIO Press Inc, New York
https://www.diopress.com

This book is part of the *Critical Pedagogies* Series

Series Editor: Shirley R. Steinberg

COVER IMAGE CRYSTAL KAMOROFF

Crystal Kamoroff is a San Francisco-based artist who has exhibited work in galleries and various art venues both nationally and throughout the Bay Area. She received her BFA from San Jose State University and MFA from Bowling Green State University. Crystal currently teaches as an adjunct instructor at Merritt College and also at the Randall Museum. Crystal is an active studio artist with a background in ceramics and sculpture, and has a passion for installation and site-specific art. She is constantly researching information and techniques that inform her work, as well as seeking out artist communities that facilitate creative dialogue and collaboration.

I dedicate this book to my dad,
who taught me the most important lesson in life:
"The only thing you can truly give someone else is attention."

Table of Contents

Preface

By Bryan Brown, Ph.D., Stanford University

There is a famous picture of Gloria Steinem and Dorothy Pitman Hughes that has been said to represent the best in feminism. There they are, two cultural icons standing shoulder-to-shoulder, raising their hands with clutched fists to merge messages of sisterhood and Black power. What a beautiful sight! This imagined world where women from all different types of backgrounds gather their voices to fight the duelling oppressors of gender bias and racism shines as a vision of what is possible. However, time has revealed a different narrative. Even as women continue to experience discrimination, violence, and mistreatment, it has been argued that the gains that women have made in the past 40 years have been granted to primarily White women. In this way, a fallacy of sisterhood has shaped the contemporary feminist justice movement, which encourages us to think about what solidarity and inclusion mean when enacted in our schools, as they are part and parcel of these over-arching narratives.

In fact, Rachel Cargale (2018) calls current feminist rhetoric "White supremacy in heels." The suggestion is that when feminist perspectives are void of an explicit focus on how race intersects with sexism that they, too, reflect the tenants of White supremacy. She explains:

> It is the type of behavior that rests under the guise of feminism only as long as it is comfortable, only as long it is personally rewarding, only as long as it keeps "on brand." But if the history of this movement taught us anything, it is that intersectionality in feminism is vital. We cannot forget the ways that

P.A. Boda (ed.), Essays on Exclusion, ix–xvi.

suffragettes dismissed the voices of Black women, sending them to the backs of their marches, only for Black activists like Ida B. Wells and Anna Julia Cooper to make major moves while fighting for the vote *in tandem* with their fight for rights as Black people – ultimately shifting the shape of this country. (Cargale, 2018, emphasis in original)

Cargle's suggestion points to the history of contradiction around race and feminism. Just as the iconic image of Gloria Steinem and Dorothy Pitman Hughes represents a contradiction that highlights the distance between iconography and reality, so too does *Essays on Exclusion: Our Critical, Collective Journey Toward Equity in Education* push us to think beyond the iconic images of 'education for all' towards more critical questions of *who* can participate in these spaces, and why.

Even if this image was met with true solidarity, there are still some ideas missing and left invisible in this narrative. As we think through issues of representation in education, the intertwining influences of race, gender, disability, class, and sexuality all reside under the umbrella of intersectionality, but for many the notion of 'intersectionality' is a code word for race/gender issues – often neglecting to include the experiences of LGBTQ+ people of color, those subjected to the context of poverty, and people living with visible/invisible disabilities. If a vision of feminism without a focus on intersectionality is "White supremacy in heels," then what is a view of education that focuses on the intersection of race and gender without a nuanced inclusion of fluid sexuality, classist dynamics, and disability? *Essays on Exclusion: Our Critical, Collective Journey Toward Equity in Education* takes us on a journey through the many answers to this question by welcoming us to think about how we have developed our own identities, as well as what those identities mean for educating students that may affiliate themselves with identities that are distinctly different than the teachers that are charged to serve them.

The chapters authored by this incredible collection of thinkers offer a vision of how educators have learned, and can learn, about racial bias, patriarchal sexism, disability, and heteronormativity. These narratives are presented in tandem with also how the authors' experiences have framed their vision of what equity and participation look and feel like for education, and society more broadly. The chapters, indeed, draw a macro-narrative of the damage done by schools, while also offering solutions for healing. Through creative prose, each chapter allows the authors to paint the picture of their pathway toward a career in education. On these journeys, we learn how racism, gender norms, ableism, and homophobia serve as hurdles and pitfalls along various pathways towards success. We also learn how teaching environments are full of these impediments and what educators need to do to become more aware of their power. Most importantly, we hear stories of success and accomplishment in a world that has largely deemed these scholars as invisible. Ultimately, *Essays on Exclusion* helps us understand how and why identities matter, while pushing us to move beyond iconography towards a truer sense of inclusion for all.

Identities Matter

The beginning of the text takes the reader on an in-depth exploration of how identity matters in our educational systems based on our personal and collective experiences. Gee (2000) described identity as an analytical lens that allows people to categorize others and themselves into meaningful groupings. Whether a person is 'smart,' 'obnoxious,' or finds pride in their 'teacher' identity, the notion of multiple identities allows individuals to send messages about who we want others to understand us to be in particular contexts (Chapman & Feldman, 2016; Gee, 2000). On the one hand, identities also allow us to recognize who a person is when compared to our own; while on the other, identities provide us a method to communicate who we would expect people to see us as in relation to our humanity, our positionality. Thus, identities have power in shaping and renegotiating the implicit and explicit messages of "who" we are.

In education, messages of teacher identity are far too often left on the margins. Teachers and teacher educators are often seen as dispensable factors to the shaping of current educational systems, and toward achieving the promise of equity in these contexts. As generations of students are greeted by educators from diverse backgrounds, our scholarship has, unfortunately, underestimated the impact of teacher identity and its impact in modern classrooms. Though every interpretation, word, and decision about how to teach is deeply entrenched in the biases and histories of teachers, we think of teachers as interchangeable – as tools that serve a singular purpose of homogenized teaching and learning as par excellence for all.

The truth is that teachers, and researchers for that matter, are humans whose histories and lived experiences can bias and/or empower them to view their students from a particular lens. *Essays on Exclusion* begins by recentering the identities of scholars as the foundation of their work. The first few chapters use conversational prose to tell the stories of how scholars can find their voice despite being marginalized. It is through these narratives that we learn how educational spaces can become the site of marginalization instead of sites of inspiration. Despite those challenges, *Essays on Exclusion* frames our schools as designed spaces for educating and identity-making, as promising contexts of hope where paths toward equity in education can be seeded and flourish when designed relationally.

Schools, Spaces, & Identity Making

Phillip A. Boda initiates the conversation by returning to the art of storytelling. The initial chapter sets the stage of the text by exploring how telling the stories of educators helps to provide a vision of what is possible in education. Boda explains,

> In turn, this book chooses to take up narrative as a site where lived experiences exist, and where identity is created, sustained, taught, challenged, and performed. This situates the nature of these experiences as social positions that can shed light onto unfamiliar realities, which some may never have purview.

His notion that the value of narratives about lived experience can provide the reader with a revelation about ways to identify and disrupt homogenized rhetoric and realities of inequity in education stands as the foundation for the text. The message is that access to equitable education for all starts by understanding who is included in the "all."

Along the same lines, the second chapter from Felicia Moore Mensah and Phillip Boda uses conversation to explore the intersections of identity and belonging. It is this early chapter where the authors begin to push the envelope on the intersecting roles of race and gender. Dr. Mensah explores how gender in scholarship enabled her a space to find her own voice in a community with few like her own. She elaborates:

> Yes, gender is important, but there are many other aspects of my identity also working together to help me understand my experiences so that I could understand the experiences of teachers I was working with. How can I talk about my identities collectively because it's not really easy to separate them out? Positional identities have to do with the intersectionality of multiple social markers that shape how we see ourselves, and specifically how we see ourselves as teachers, while also engaging with how Self shapes how we teach and how we develop relationships with students, and with science.

It is in these early words where the text begins to take shape by exploring just how deeply identity allows us to see the world from our own lenses as a way to support others who may not align with our experiences.

As the text moves forward, it helps the reader reframe the value of 'who' teachers and scholars can be and how their identities shape their scholarship. Carefully crafted narratives by Drs. Carlos Adams and Yolanda Sealey-Ruiz tell the story of how to maintain hope despite explicit and implicit messages of exclusion. Their narratives send a resounding message that who you are is enough and will stand as the source of your excellence in the face of exclusion. Dr. Sealey-Ruiz offers the following as an exemplar of this charge:

> I write my own reality into existence in this chapter, specifically to unmask and challenge those narratives that have shaped and shaded the humanity of Black children in schools. The failure of Black students cannot be an option and teachers are the path toward this goal. Schools must create environments that reflect the racial and cultural diversity of Black students and affirm that their lives matter. Schools must be deliberate in asking if their Black students feel comfortable and safe, cared for and acknowledged. Given the history of this racist country toward Black people, extra efforts must be put forth to include, not exclude, Black and Brown youth from educational opportunities.

This powerful call for inclusion is not simply a call made from the sidelines. Rather, Sealey-Ruiz tells the story of how 'who' she is as a scholar enabled her to develop an intimate understanding of exclusionary practices in schools. The deep knowledge shared by these educator-scholars provides the reader with a vision of what schools could become when we actively work against exclusion and include the powerful voices from the margins.

Learning Racism & Homophobia

The book then takes on a unique third layer as its next stanza pushes the boundaries of what counts as intersectionality. Kimberlee Crenshaw's (1989) seminal work on intersectionality has become the theory of choice recently. Standing shoulder to shoulder with feminist perspectives like Standpoint Theory that argue people from the margins gain additional layers of insight because they must view the world from so many different lenses to survive (Harding, 1997; 2004), Crenshaw's notion of intersectionality provides scholars with a lens to explain the compounding influences of race, class, and gender.

Crenshaw explained, "This focus on the most privileged group members marginalizes those who are multiply-burdened, and obscures claims that cannot be understood as resulting from discrete sources of discrimination" (1989 p. 140). In this case, she argued that a focus on White females created a differential burden for those who are positioned and are affected by bias because they are African-American and female. In explaining how African-American women were left out of the conversation in terms of civil rights, Crenshaw elaborates on how laws intended to fight gender discrimination prioritized White women, and thus sacrificed African-American women under the guise of gender equity.

Essays on Exclusion pushes the borders of intersectionality to suggest that when the term is taken up by scholars, its adoption can overlook notions of sexuality, class, and disability identity that are lost in discussions of an intersectional gaze focused solely on race and gender. Specifically, Boda discusses how homophobia is learned at school and serves to push people to the margins of education, across disciplines, in the most un-American of ways. He explains,

> This consequence, again, is learned, not inherent in the fabric of what it means to be human, or what it means to be a citizen of a nation-state, such as being 'American.' Indeed, if we define 'American' as a constitutionalist would, we all have the right to life, liberty, and the pursuit of happiness without the threat of outside imposition.

The subsequent chapter by Reid and Devereaux calls for the explicit recognition of this new layer of intersectional engagement. They challenge us to reconstruct what counts as normal such that we do not allow children to suffer the fate of invisibility that occurs when one recognizes racial oppression but fails to identify the oppression of queer communities in spaces fighting for social justice. They explain this positionality in-depth for the reader using vignettes from their lived experiences:

> I had already been in circles that chose to not to see me: White folks who never really tried to get to know me, either assuming that they already did or not concerning themselves with idea that they didn't; White girls who exoticized me; White women who pitied my Blackness and assumed I yearned for their Whiteness; Black boys who saw my body, but only saw my body; Black men who valued the voices of other men the most... Yes, I had been unnoticed and unseen. I didn't like how it felt, but I learned not to expect more from them.

Chapters 5 (Drs. Nusbaum et al.) and 6 (Dr. Powell) further this conversation on invisibility, tokenism, and realities that intersectional identities face in schools, specifically addressing the pervasive nature of disability justice within and between institutional structures, as well as the effect heteronormativity can have when juxtaposed with Blackness in educational contexts. These powerful narratives of the unseen – the 'ontologically erased' in Nusbaum et al.'s words – help to set the foundation for the final group of chapters in the text where readers are asked to consider what they can do to work against the injustice of exclusionary practices across disciplines. In turn, the final section of *Essays on Exclusion* points the reader to potential solutions – problematizing philosophical, epistemological, and pragmatic methods of exclusion.

Reframing & 'Revolutionizing' Identities in Education, and Beyond

The last section in the text offers a sense of hope through praxis as the narratives told provide a blueprint for the possibilities of moving forward toward equity in radically intersectional ways. In Chapter 8, Drs. ReAnna Roby and Angela Calabrese-Barton, along with their collaborating student authors, suggest that educators use a more communal approach to counteract exclusion by integrating students' narratives in STEM (science, technology, engineering, and mathematics) spaces. They explain,

> Through not only sharing the narratives of youth within this work, but also co-authoring, we look to disrupt the dominant discourses that exclude Black girls from STEM and making, to see the ways in which their participation yields one of inclusivity and resistance – both socially and politically.

Their work offers a vision of the potential benefits of layering student's identity into the design of STEM learning environments. They suggest a call to arms for educators to build curriculum that intentionally construct spaces for inclusion in STEM environments, and arguably beyond.

This final section of the book also offers a framework to problematize binary perspectives of identity (Chapter 9, Dr. AnaLouise Keating), toward a more dynamic lens for intersectional spaces that also considers the notion of stranger-making (Chapter 7, Dr. Debbie Sonu). Indeed, Roby & Calabrese Barton's Chapter 8 on making in STEM also helps to provide a vision of what inclusive disciplinary spaces might look and feel like. Taken together, these last three chapters suggest that scholars can no longer see disciplinary spaces as contexts where the lives of women – in all their intersectional beauty – are not integrated, leveraged, and valued; rather, they argue, along with other authors in this volume, that the space itself must be *designed* as a site for the liberation of diverse positionalities from the hegemony of the banking system of education emphasizing homogenized teaching and learning. In sum, these authors help us push beyond notions of iconography toward the construction of spaces, and interactions, that empower and name the intersections between identity, narrative, and equitable disciplinary learning.

The question that emerges after reading *Essays on Exclusion* is what would true inclusion looks like? It would certainly be more nuanced than the image of Gloria Steinem and Dorothy Pitman Hughes. In fact, the mere assumption that a photograph could represent inclusion undermines just how detailed intersectionality can be in education and society more broadly. Therefore, if feminism without a focus on race is "White supremacy in heels," then an intersectional vision of education without a vision for class, gender, disability, and sexual identity presents an exclusionary paradigm that welcomes some while concurrently pushing others to the margins by design rather than happenstance. A future for equity in education is one that must include everyone, in all the messy and beautiful ways humanity is embodied among diverse stakeholders and the children they seek to serve. *Essays on Exclusion* pushes this vision forward by calling for an awakening throughout the educational world across all disciplines. I believe it is time to listen closely to what these scholars have to say; if not for our own betterment, for all of our children's.

Bryan A. Brown, Ph.D.

References

Cargle, R. E. (2018, August 16). When feminism Is White supremacy in heels. Retrieved May 21, 2019, from Harper's BAZAAR website: https://www.harpersbazaar.com/culture/politics/a22717725/what-is-toxic-white-feminism/

Chapman, A., & Feldman, A. (2016). Cultivation of science identity through authentic science in an urban high school classroom. *Cultural Studies of Science Education*, 1–23. https://doi.org/10.1007/s11422-015-9723-3

Crenshaw, K. (1989). Demarginalizing the intersection of race and sex: A Black feminist critique of antidiscrimination doctrine, feminist theory and antiracist politics. *University of Chicago Legal Forum*, *1989*, 139–168.

Gee, J. P. (2000). Identity as an analytic lens for research in education. *Review of Research in Education*, *25*, 99–125. https://doi.org/10.2307/1167322

Harding, S. (1997). Comment on Hekman's "Truth and method: Feminist standpoint theory revisited": Whose standpoint needs the regimes of truth and reality? *Signs: Journal of Women in Culture and Society*, *22*, 382–391. https://doi.org/10.1086/495163

Harding, S. (2004). *The feminist standpoint theory reader: Intellectual and political controversies*. Psychology Press.

Introduction

PART ONE

PHILLIP A. BODA

Narrating Others

It happened as I was leaving an elementary classroom that I had just
collected data in; the students had just experienced a virtual reality science
lesson designed using tenets of culturally relevant pedagogy (i.e., designed
to foster a disciplinary-related cultural competency and a context-specific
sociopolitical awareness; Ladson-Billings, 1995). The students were asked
by their teacher to come back to the rug while I collected our research
group's materials and was headed out the door, duffle bag in tow. The
teacher stopped the class to have them say thank you to me for bringing
this unique technologically-enhanced learning experience to their class, and
what ensued encouraged me to think more deeply about how context
influences our perceptions of ourselves and others.

> Teacher: Class, let's say thank you to Dr. Boda for coming into our class
> today.
>
> Students (all together): Thank you, Mr. Boda.
>
> Teacher: No, no, his name is *Dr.* Boda.
>
> Students (in unison, again): Thank you Mr. Dr. Boda.
>
> [I smile and chuckle a bit, knowing full well the innocence of their
> mislabeling]
>
> Teacher: Dr. Boda isn't a medical doctor, he's a professor, like at a
> university
>
> [I smile again, knowing I am not a professor but a postdoctoral researcher –
> they didn't need to know the difference yet; their understanding of

hierarchal designations need not be nuanced to the levels of authority that often permeate higher education pomp and circumstance]

A single Brown boy stands up at his place on the rug with confidence, chin in the air

Boy: He looks like a professor.

The Black and Brown boys surrounding him concur: Yeah he does!

[I gushed – and probably blushed – I had never felt so valued and happy to represent the professorate because, in the eyes of these Black and Brown children, I was something that they could be one day: I was a model, an identity they could see themselves embodying, and I set an example – it, too, was possible for them to be a professor].

This excerpt, like the many others you will read in this book, are glimpses into the lives of the authors and the people they love – indeed, they are revealing and transparent. In this way, I wanted to start this introduction with a disclaimer, a request: The authors in this volume have put their souls into their writing so, please, as you read through this book defer judgment, dampen any urge to generalize their experiences, and thoughtfully listen – truly listen – to how and in what ways the authors frame the stories they tell about exclusion. I believe the task of any educator, administrator, researcher, or policymaker is to first and foremost do no harm and that requires a keen eye toward knowing when to listen. Moving forward, we will be discussing many different lived realities, both from the perspective of the person them self and through indirect analysis – the vicarious second-hand, but no less valuable, restorying of the lives of those that have been subjected to Othering (Dussel, 1999). In this way, I wanted to also start this book with a background on what narrative and experience have to do with equity in education, as well as how stories told from the position of the person being excluded can be considered as advantageous resources for those in education to engage with, if we seek to work toward a collective goal of disrupting educational inequity and exclusion.

Part I of the introduction begins with a background on narrative and experience from a point of view that deconstructs the importance of culture in how we narrate Others. Part 2 then transitions into a dialogue with Dr. Felicia Moore Mensah about these topics to engage the reader with a way to take up an analysis of the chapters of this book, specifically interrogating how we narrate ourselves. Through these components, it is proposed that the reader can start to take up the task of excavating their own experiences, as well as generate a more critical understanding of how particular narratives developed out of those experiences frame their perceptions of people in particular contexts. In doing so, the reader can begin the task of starting to unpack their understandings of positionality (Mensah, 2016) and we can move toward a theory of exclusion that is both inclusive of differing realities that those affected by exclusion face, as well as shed light onto where we can shift to attack head-on the task of designing equity for all.

On Narrative and Experience

> To say that an identity is socially constructed is to say not that it does not refer to anything in reality, but that what it refers to is a contingent product of social negotiations rather than a natural kind. (Martin-Alcoff, 2004, p.320)

Linda Martin-Alcoff's quote rings all too true for those doing equity work – it speaks to the contextualization of identity but also the construction of that identity as interplaying between Self and Other. Oftentimes when we talk about narrative and experience, we want to parse out the essences of those personal realities. However, to the teacher in the classroom or administrator working toward setting up systems in their school to improve academic success this approach sometimes falls short due to its philosophical commitments that shade the realities that these stakeholders are trying to grapple with on a daily basis. In turn, this book chooses to take up narrative as a site where lived experiences exist, and where identity is created, sustained, taught, challenged, and performed. This situates the nature of these experiences as social positions that can shed light onto unfamiliar realities, which some may never have purview. Within shifting from the margin (personal narrative) to center (macro-narratives) (hooks, 2000), personal experience and the narratives that emerge from them are seen as valuable processes and products that highlight those forgotten through multiple marginalization (Annamma, 2017) and the nature of included exclusion (Boda, 2018). These narratives then become artifacts of the ways personal experience and macro-narratives interact.

In other words, this book conceptualizes narrative as a story that is being told through the perspective of the person who lived it and, in taking this conception of narrative seriously, it resists the urge to impose solely our interpretations (our own meanings) onto the story being told. This framing of narrative starts to re-center the reality that stories have power – for the personal, the interpersonal, and the political. This book, by taking up this standpoint, seeks to reframe narrative, experience, and stories as glimpses into how equity can be taken up as an intersectional praxis (Crenshaw, 1991) – to move beyond siphoned and siloed singular explanations of identity and its impact to how people think and learn about themselves and Others. While educational research has long relegated personal stories and narrative into the realm of the individual experience, this volume's purpose is to, instead, focus on the value and promise of narrative and experience to explore how contexts, such as those in education, shape the preferential status of some people while devaluing others – the premise, process, and sustainment of exclusion.

One such narrative by Gloria Anzaldúa exemplifies such a task, and request, by exposing and making transparent the importance of experience, showcasing how exclusion and inclusion operate relationally (1999, p.43). In her description of her Chicana identity, Anzaldúa describes how she had little exposure to Whiteness before her high school and graduate school, as well as reflects on what that meant when she brought her particular positionality (as a woman of color with Mexican heritage) to these spaces. Through the self-excavation of her experiences, Gloria Anzaldúa provides for us a base from which a discussion on positionality can be had in relation to narrative, as well as its importance for understanding its impact on teaching and learning. I have done a similar reflexive exercise below, drawing from my mixed-race(d), queer, and male positions to situate my own positionality:

> My mixed-raced identity is grounded in the interaction of each side of my identity – the White one and the Brown – within primarily White American contexts, where to be included meant you had to act like everyone else. I have been ostracized from Brown contexts because I was 'too White,' as well as from White contexts for being 'the only Brown boy in the classroom.' Like many other mixed-race people in America, trying to find where we 'fit' is an everchanging puzzle piece that changes based on where we live. I oftentimes find myself at odds with the fact that I grew up White – I never lived in a context where Brown identities were valued and, in turn, never saw a person of color as a teacher – as a model to look up to – until I was in my undergraduate degree. These experiences informed how I viewed these normalized representations, and what it meant for someone like me who could not 'fit' into these nice, neat boxes. I understood early on I must live with both my Brown and White self, that I have to think about what it means to be mixed-race(d) in particular contexts, and I have to be vigilant as to how my queerness is read by those in contexts where to 'be myself' may mean I am subjected to physical, psychological, and spiritual harm – an experience that I am all too familiar with.

Indeed, the above exercise should help the reader to see the importance of understanding how changing of personal attributes (race, gender, and the like) shifts the nature of how the experience is narrated. If we take up this exercise for a White, heterosexual, cis-gendered man, the narrative would change, undoubtedly. In this hypothetical narrative, this White man may not reference their race, sexuality, or gender as impacting how they have been treated growing up because their community (the White heterosexual community) sees their positionality as the norm – they do not need to excavate or question their existence as being a deviation from the norm: they are accepted for who they are in those contexts unquestionably. Granted, as communities continue to diversify, America is embarking on an era where it must face the original premises of 'a melting-pot society' being of a specific kind of assimilation, especially in relation to who previously (and currently) benefits the most from the continued support of these perceived, normalized positionalities.

It is here, in the tenuous space between the margins and center, that exclusion and inclusion operate, while this borderland between the norm and the subaltern continually shifts based on context. For example, when I traveled to Europe for the first time, I observed an interesting phenomenon. When I spoke English in my initial requests to French citizens, I was responded to less than favorably; however, when I used the minimal Spanish I knew to ask questions, these same citizens responded favorably with a smile and request to speak in English. This was a case where to try to connect between differing social capitals – the attributes that help people find a sense of belonging and support within particular contexts – my charge was to shift my focus not on who I was as a person, per say, but rather how I approach the nature of my position as an American in a foreign land – as an enacted positionality in context.

This experience tasked me with understanding the ways that would be conducive for me to connect favorably with people I was unlike and then leverage that knowledge of cultural capital – the attributes valued by people in a context based on their geo-historical and bio-political realities (Mignolo, 2011) – such that both parties felt comfortable engaging in the process of transacting capital. This type of distinction is not unfamiliar to those critical scholars in education; Emdin (2011) provides a refreshing look into how the difference between interaction and transaction takes place at the level of the teacher-student discourse. Through these articulations, through these stories that exemplify that personal experience frames how we see ourselves and Others, we find a path to engaging with narrative as not merely a 'story' but as a mirror into the realities that people face, which allows us to start to engage ourselves as participants in this cultural phenomenon of reading ourselves and others.

To say that identity plays a role in how people understand themselves and others should be unquestionably apparent given our current political climate; however, even with the recognition that we react differently to people whether they are similar or different from our own positionality, we cannot forget that this rhetorical and theoretical premise affects material realities. In other words, as we move to understand ourselves as products of contexts that create affiliation or alienation (Emdin, 2010), we must also think critically about how the narratives around identity shade our perceptions of what positionalities are valued in particular contexts such as education, and, in doing so, both look back and look forward to frame this conjecture and process of 'becoming' as a function of both personal experience and the contexts that bore and bred that story. One such powerful narrative is concerned with 'street culture' or 'hip-hop.'

Multiple Perspectives Toward Narrating Others

As an outsider looking in, hip-hop, along with other forms of culture such as Zoot suits and hydraulic switches on cars in the Chican@ community, may be assumed to be examples of reasons why Black and Brown students don't succeed – these contexts are seen as more of a detriment to their success than a support, from this viewpoint, because they deviate from the White norm of 'Being.' However, what we should garner from the narratives told in music – these stories of lived reality – is that the nature of the context in which hip-hop artists grow up is, in fact, very different from the narratives being told about the White experience in suburban America. These storytellers provide a glimpse of some of the layers that they faced growing up, but also provide an alternative narrative in relation to how they are reflecting on those realities – speaking 'truth' to power.

It is not enough to argue that these stories are detrimental to Black and Brown youth because they showcase only the negative aspects of these artists' lives growing up – this superficial reading is, of course, grounded in a colonial logic of similarity to the norm that justifies appropriateness and acceptability (Oliver, 2004). A more thorough, critical reading would also tease out the nuances of how these artists recognize and make apparent that the capitalist mindset for success – unbridled materialism and bootstrap ideology – is a significant pressure into the reasons if, how, and why youth living in similar contexts that suffer from poverty may be subject to exclusion in relation to the larger White society's hypervigilance and hyper policing of communities of color, subsequently placing them into the prison industrial complex because of this perceived deviance, delinquency, and criminality (Barnes & Motz, 2018; Skiba, Arredondo, & Williams, 2014). This turn of analysis is one of recognizing one's own positionality in relation to the narrative being told; it is not an insignificant task to do, nor is it an easily understood shift given the history of stories told of and about people of color. Indeed, the often-lauded critique of hip-hop, siphoning the stories told into singular analyses of its misogyny and criminal elements, have been challenged elsewhere by eminent cultural theorist bell hooks, who provided an eloquent response to this myopic viewing of the cultural phenomenon of 'gangsta rap' out of context (1994, p. 115–116, 122).

Hip-hop, then, as a cultural product is subjected to a restorying of its purpose as being an indication, nay justification, that mirrors neocolonial rhetoric that emphasizes anything that differs from the 'civilized' and 'safe' White norm to be barbaric, primitive, and inferior. hooks (1994) also illuminates the nature of how and why this perceived deficit – of Blackness as less than – is continually under surveillance by those (White and Black) that perceive this cultural phenomenon as detrimental. This use of rhetoric and construed propaganda to story the lives of those subjected to exclusion (in this case Blackness, in general, and deviation from White cultural values more specifically) also shapes and shades how teachers, administrators, and policymakers take up how to support students because of its impact on the types of representations seen by these stakeholders in relation to Blackness, class, and urban contexts.

In turn, Christopher Emdin (2016) has called for a reframing of youth of color as the neoindigenous to better explain the experiences that poor youth of color face when they walk into classrooms where an imposed neocolonial logic of sameness is used as justification to deny them a place and space to express their cultural capital in ways that are valued and leveraged to help them learn. This expression and performance of sameness as value – as Whiteness as property (Annamma, 2015; Harris, 1992; Mensah & Jackson, 2018) – permeates our educational system, its policies and procedures. Therefore, to take up the task of pursuing equity in education, teachers, administrators, and policymakers must also become cognizant of their own relational positions and those subjected to Othering, to once more center narrative as an artifact of injustice and listen to the experiences that shape exclusion's multiple faces.

But what does this mean for education? Principally, this type of analysis aids teachers to understand the identities students take up in classrooms that look and feel similar to previous contexts that have excluded them in the past, as well as describes the nature of power that is held within that discernment of Self and Other. Another experience related to the act of narrating others speaks to this idea:

> It's my second-year teaching in Brooklyn. The elevator opens to an after-hours session – late night for me. I look up from my coffee and there he is, one of my students that had consistently donned a 'street' identity in my class, both in his anti-school discourse and lackadaisical approach to schoolwork [conservative media may use the label 'thug' but I do not]. He's a hefty young man, short and stout but today was different: He was crying, bewildered to say the least. I start to talk with him, immediately trying to find out what brought him to tears – the identity he employed on a daily basis would never permit this type of vulnerability, especially not in front of persons of authority. He told me how teachers and administration were trying to transfer him and I knew then that the positioning of him as 'disruptive' and 'hood' had taken its toll – the self-fulfilled prophesy that many of his teachers had emboldened in the ways they spoke and interacted with him had produced a materiality of harm, a physical and emotional exclusion that bore scars so vivid that they burst out of him at this moment. We talked a bit more and it was all I could do to just hug him, to tell him I'm here for him and will fight for him ... He ended up finishing his high school tenure at that school shaking his hand as he walked across the stage at graduation. Proud.

Students like this one we write off all the time, whether through consistent conflict between their (perceived and performed) positionality and the unexamined assumptions that teachers hold about what 'good' (Broderick & Leonardo, 2016) or 'smart' (Hatt, 2012) students are in these White schooling contexts. This type of analysis, as will be argued throughout this book, requires that we be open to understanding the stories youth tell themselves about who they are, as well as who they are in relation to others and the normative center of schools (Leonardo & Broderick, 2011). To become aware of such a metacognitive analysis, we need alternative explanations of life; stakeholders in education who have never experienced anything beyond the White heterosexual capitalist patriarchy need new narratives to help them understand how and in what ways they own personal experience influences the expected norms from their students, as well as how the cultural capital they hold for themselves dictates for them (and subsequently for their students) what academic achievement entails (Aronson & Laughter, 2016).

To do so means to reframe our understandings of how we narrate the experiences of others through our own lenses (our own referential frames defined by our experiences), and, inevitably, as we conduct such an unpacking of our own positionality, we find how the narratives we tell ourselves about who and what are valuable in particular contexts shape and shade the stories we convince ourselves about Others that differ from that position. The next part to this introduction is an interview between Dr. Felicia Moore Mensah and I, which provides a model for engaging with narrative and positionality in context – one that deconstructs the nature and function of Narrating Ourselves so that readers can get a glimpse as what this process may look like in practice. Through this dialogue, it is proposed that the reader will gain another layer of interaction with the text, as well as providing a method to move beyond analysis toward taking up a critical eye toward their own classrooms, the educational system more broadly, and the nature of how we produce knowledge.

References

Annamma, S. A. (2015). Whiteness as property: Innocence and ability in teacher education. *The Urban Review*, 47, 293-316.

Annamma, S. A. (2017). *The pedagogy of pathologization: Dis/abled girls of color in the school-prison nexus*. Routledge.

Anzaldúa, G. (1999). *Borderlands/La Frontera*. San Francisco: Aunt Lute.

Aronson, B., & Laughter, J. (2016). The theory and practice of culturally relevant education: A synthesis of research across content areas. *Review of Educational Research*, 86, 163-206.

Barnes, J. C., & Motz, R. T. (2018). Reducing racial inequalities in adulthood arrest by reducing inequalities in school discipline: Evidence from the school-to-prison pipeline. *Developmental Psychology*, 54, 2328-2340.

Boda, P. A. (2018). Exclusion from participation in science: Confessions from an ally on the other side of the fence. In M. Koomen, S. Kahn, C. Atchison, & T. Wild (Eds.), *Toward inclusion of all learners through science teacher education* (pp. 301-314). Brill/Sense Publishing.

Broderick, A., & Leonardo, Z. (2016). What a good boy: The deployment and distribution of "goodness" as ideological property in schools. In D. J. Connor, B. A. Ferri, & S. A. Annamma (Eds.), *DisCrit – Disability Studies and Critical Race Theory in education*, (pp. 55-67). New York, NY: Teachers College Press.

Crenshaw, K. (1991). Mapping the margins: Identity politics, intersectionality, and violence against women. *Stanford Law Review*, 43, 1241-1299.

Dussel, E. (1999). "Sensibility" and "Otherness" in Emmanuel Levinas. *Philosophy Today*, 43, 126-134.

Emdin, C. (2010). Affiliation and alienation: Hip-hop, rap, and urban science education. *Journal of Curriculum Studies*, 42(1), 1-25.

Emdin, C. (2011). Dimensions of communication in urban science education: Interactions and transactions. *Science Education*, 95(1), 1-20.

Emdin, C. (2016). *For White folks who teach in the hood... and the rest of y'all too: Reality pedagogy and urban education*. Beacon Press.

Hatt, B. (2012). Smartness as a cultural practice in schools. *American Educational Research Journal*, 49, 438-460.

Harris, C. I. (1993). Whiteness as property. *Harvard Law Review*, 106, 1707–1791.

hooks, b. (1994). *Outlaw culture*. New York: Routledge.

hooks, b. (2000). *Feminist theory: From margin to center*. Pluto Press.

Ladson-Billings, G. (1995). Toward a theory of culturally relevant pedagogy. *American*

Educational Research Journal, 32, 465-491.

Leonardo, Z., & Broderick, A. (2011). Smartness as property: A critical exploration of intersections between Whiteness and disability studies. *Teachers College Record,* 113, 2206-2232.

Martin-Alcoff, L. (2004). Is Latina/o identity a racial identity? In J. J. Gracia & E. Millán-Zaibert (Eds.), *Latin American philosophy for the 21st century: The human condition, values, and the search for identity* (p. 311-334). Amherst, NY: Prometheus Books.

Mensah F.M. (2016) Positional identity as a framework to studying science teacher identity. In L. Avraamidou (Ed.), *Studying science teacher identity: New directions in mathematics and science education* (p.49-69). Rotterdam, The Netherlands: Sense Publishing.

Mensah, F. M., & Jackson, I. (2018). Whiteness as property in science teacher education. *Teachers College Record,* 120, 1-38.

Mignolo, W. D. (2011). Geopolitics of sensing and knowing: on (de) coloniality, border thinking and epistemic disobedience. *Postcolonial Studies,* 14, 273-283.

Oliver, K. (2004). *The colonization of psychic space: A psychoanalytic social theory of oppression.* U of Minnesota Press.

Skiba, R. J., Arredondo, M. I., & Williams, N. T. (2014). More than a metaphor: The contribution of exclusionary discipline to a school-to-prison pipeline. *Equity & Excellence in Education,* 47, 546-564.

INTRODUCTION

PART TWO

FELICIA MOORE MENSAH & PHILLIP A. BODA

Narrating Ourselves

Phillip Boda (PB): Could we start off by telling a little bit of background about yourself; you know the volume has a lot of different perspectives coming in, so what brought you to education and education research?

Felicia Moore Mensah (FM): I started education not really coming into it on purpose. In college I was a pre-med major, I wanted to go to medical school, and some of that was part of my family saying 'oh you're going to be a doctor' because I liked science and math. Another reason was that my mother had always been ill growing up and I didn't think her doctors were treating her well. I thought, 'Well I need to go to medical school, and I can treat my momma.'

I liked the sciences, I grew up in rural North Carolina, so I was always playing around, more or less, with nature. You would think I would major in environmental science, but I was a biology major because that's what I thought doctors majored in when they went off to college. I liked the subject area and had always done well in the sciences and math when I was in high school, as well as when I went to college, except for organic chemistry. Even after finishing my undergraduate college years, I was still a pre-med major and I got to the end of my program and I didn't really want to go to medical school; I didn't have the strongest desire like I had before. Some of that were the influences of being a science major and hearing a lot of negativity akin to exclusion, like, 'Black women can't become doctors,' 'It's going to be really hard for you to be a doctor,' and 'All this time it's going to take' – there was a lot of negativity and I didn't

P.A. Boda (ed.), Essays on Exclusion, 11-20.

have anything positive encouraging me to go into medicine. I then attended a program at UNC Chapel Hill for students of color who wanted to go to medical school. They had Black medical school mentors for us to work with, and it was during the summer. That was the first time I saw any Black people in the sciences in terms of going into medical school.

I was at the end of my program and I thought, 'Well, what else can I do.' Genetics was the area I was most interested in, and I thought 'perhaps I'll get my bachelor's degree in genetics and I would become a genetics counselor, or something related to that.' I was going to go to MIT [Massachusetts Institute of Technology]. But just like selecting my undergraduate institution, my family didn't have any money, and I didn't have any money to go to MIT. I decided to attend an HBCU [Historically Black College and University] because I had an aunt who was an alum of North Carolina A&T [Agricultural & Technical] in Greensboro. She said I could come and live with her and my uncle while I go to graduate school. It wasn't very far from home in Selma, versus going to MIT where it was far away, and I didn't have any money or anywhere to live.

I felt good going to NC A&T. It is a good institution. It was completely opposite from my time in Chapel Hill. Chapel Hill was predominantly White with a little bit of the elitism of the private Ivy leagues. I figured I would have a change and go to my people. I would go to an HBCU. And it was a very welcoming environment. I had the experience of undergraduate education, so I felt comfortable in this type of school context. They wanted bright people of color to come to the institution and, at the time, they had a fairly good science department.

I worked in a science lab teaching and also worked in the psychology department as a researcher. Both of these were great experiences for me. I thought I would have a career in the lab. In my undergraduate years, I worked for a doctor, a cardiologist, in his lab. As I was working on my thesis project, I ran into issues. This is where gender comes into play. I actually had a Black male – well, all my professors at the time were Black males, older men, but one in particular was my thesis advisor – and he was not very supportive. He didn't really help me in the lab, just kind of left me by myself. I had to figure out a lot of things on my own and it just wasn't a good fit for me. I finished all my course work, but I needed to complete the research project that focused on his work with reproduction using horseshoe crabs. I spoke with the Dean of the Graduate School, and I told him of the challenges I was having, which he noted were concerns he had heard previously. I came to get my degree, so what else can I do? He said I can go into education.

I was like 'I don't want to go into education' because I had never thought about it. My fear was standing in front of people and talking, and I didn't want everyone looking at me. In the lab, you were kind of by yourself. I decided to face my fear. I took a semester off to work and then I went back into the Master's program for teaching. Teaching was not my intention. I took my first couple education classes and I loved it. Though I finished my degree in education, I didn't get certified. I still wanted to work in the lab so I worked for Procter and Gamble in a microbiology lab.

I had a friend who said their school system needed science teachers and she thought, with my background in science, I would be a really good science teacher. Long story short, I left the lab and went into the classroom. My first teaching position was in Charlotte, North Carolina. I taught biology, physical science, and earth science. Teaching science and being in the classroom is where everything came together for me. I was creative, I was imaginative, and I was able to take difficult concepts and make them engaging and easy to learn.

Thinking about the topic of your book, I did not feel excluded. I really felt like the classroom was mine and I could do whatever I wanted to do and so a lot of the things I saw in terms of people not having access to science, I thought I could build into my classroom teaching and the curriculum so that *all* students would be included in the sciences. All that I do in education as an educator is to be inclusive because my experiences have not always been inclusive.

PB: I understand that a lot. Similarly, I went from the sciences to education within my first year of undergraduate education and graduated with a B.S. in Education; that's a lot of our narratives in science education. Thinking about all of these past experiences, how do you think it frames your current identity as an education researcher; how does it help you think about what your role is?

FM: As a researcher, I have done work in many areas and all that I have done shapes my current narrative. Maintaining the strength I have as a Black woman, I take this with me everywhere I go. I try to. I want to be in spaces where I can be authentically me and be accepted in those spaces. Oftentimes there are spaces where I am the only person of color present. Most of the time, you probably have heard this and experienced it as well, where people say you have to be the representative of everybody. In some ways I think yes, I do because I – we – haven't been represented in a lot of places, and I feel like I have to be there to represent everybody. Not that my narrative is going to be the same as everybody, or that I can honestly represent all Black people, or all females, or all Black females, but being there and speaking up for that particular moment, as the only person of color or female person of color at the table, then I have to represent those who are not there.

PB: Absolutely. I think when you talk about all your previous experiences with mentors and in the classroom, it makes me think about if you have any experiences as a teacher that stands out in terms of how you think about your work now in relation to identity and positionality – do you look back and say 'oh, that's what was really happening there'?

FM: Yes, but I think coming into education at the particular level of your doctorate, you start to see theory and practice. But I have always had practice and I always had theory. I just didn't know what it was called. So, yes, I can look back at the things that I've done, and it has a name, a theory to help explain my practice. For example, all this time, I was doing multiculturalism or culturally relevant teaching and I didn't know that was what I was doing. I was focused on the experiences that my students brought into the classroom. I was making the content connect with them, getting them excited about learning science, and understanding concepts.

PB: Speaking to your research and working with teachers, in the book the authors really focus on narrative as a vehicle to describe how exclusion operates and I'm wondering if you could describe if and in what ways narrative has informed your own work with teachers.

FM: Narrative was one of the frameworks that I used for my dissertation study. I see narrative as telling stories, and hearing from others, and wanting to know what people's experiences are like. As I find out what people's stories are, then I'm able to write about them, while subsequently learning about them in more depth. The narratives of teachers and the work they do is really important for me to try to understand – 'How did you come to be the teacher you say you want to be' or 'what were your ideas when you entered the classroom,' 'what kind of teacher did you want to be' – just trying to understand their background and how that plays a major role in how they look at their students and how they think about the content, if they're teaching. Do they even know or think about how their past experiences are informing their current practices? Really trying to have that conversation, that narrative, come out. And to see how to put theory on top of all of that.

I've always seen practice and theory together. So sometimes in education they say there's this practice/theory divide, but I've never seen them divided. It's hard for me to say what it was before now, how did they work separately? I've always seen them together and I want teachers to see that as well; looking at their stories to say, 'Yes, I'm applying this particular theory to what I'm doing,' and then asking, 'Do you understand why you are doing that or do you understand why it's not working?'

As a doctoral student and sometimes in my early work with teachers, they often did things in their classrooms, but didn't understand why it did not work. I see this all the time still as I'm working in classrooms. One of my favorite misunderstandings of theory and practice was with a middle school teacher and a high school teacher where the teachers said they were doing cooperative learning. I said, 'Well, tell me what cooperative learning is and how do you set up in your classroom,' and, of course, it was not what they were doing at all. Just having students talk to each to work on a worksheet is not cooperative learning. Getting them to understand the theory behind it and being able to change some practices and routines, how they set up a classroom, and what roles they might play in the classroom with students was beneficial to them. Sharing the theory, practicing it, and knowing their students helped, too. But I started with helping them build upon what they were already doing and to know the theory more deeply. So, for me, talking with teachers and working with them to improve and change their practices begins with narratives.

PB: I completely agree. I think how you articulate theory and practice as sort of a symbiotic relationship is fascinating because in my experiences it's sort of different – back and forth between too much theory or too practical when I work with teachers. I loved how you described how you worked with those teachers and they thought they were doing one thing but when you start to break it down and started to get them to think why this is working or why is it not working, to get them to dig a little bit deeper, I think really hits on the purpose of the book to talk about exclusion, because we often talk about what happens after exclusion. I often wonder, what do you say to those teachers right now? So, in the book, we talk about exclusion in very broad categories and the authors bring a lot of different perspectives when they describe it. You have a lot of experience working toward equity in education and so how do you see exclusion influencing the teachers you work with?

FM: They don't know that they're excluding. I think we talk about science specifically, and it could be in other areas, but I know for sure around science, because teachers often have an underlying bias that only the best and the brightest can go into the sciences, and they treat classrooms and students that way. But they never imagine the students and their interests outside of the classroom as resources for learning science. That if they tapped into what interests them, inclusion will happen. This is also part of my personal story. I was doing so much science at home but when I came to school, it was not even mentioned. I wasn't asked about what I was doing at home to connect to what I was doing in school. I remember doing an insect project for school because I could bring stuff from home, out of my yard and from the woody areas and bring things to the classroom. But there was really not a well-defined connection between what was happening at home and what was happening in my schooling experiences. I saw it at home from doing all kinds of stuff, being curious about what I could find or play with and connect it to science for myself.

I think teachers just don't know to merely ask about children's experiences to be able to connect home to school. For science, they don't think their students may be interested in science or mathematics outside of school so they don't think they can bring those interests into classroom lessons, content, and activities. I work with teachers to say 'Well, let's find out what students' interests are.' With the elementary methods class I teach, they have to do an interview, even if it's just five minutes talking to children: What are their interests? What do you like or know about a particular science topic? And they have to take that information to plan lessons. They also have lunchtime conversations. Eating and talking with children. What do children have that we are not tapping into, that we can put into the science classroom, or any of the content areas? Science is an area you think only the best and the brightest should be engaged, and mathematics, too. But given that exclusionary bias that teachers have for marginalized children, particularly students of color, we never tap into their interests and we do not fully see the great potential in children.

PB: That brings me to your articulations of positional identity, or positionality. Could you describe a little about it and then its importance for teachers?

FM: I'm going to give you the theoretical basis because it's going to connect the things that I'm doing now in terms of my teaching and research. I came into science with a feminist lens, thinking more about gender and science. When I was in my doctoral program, I took a lot of gender and sociology classes and tried to frame gender-related theory onto what was happening in science education. When I was in my gender classes and reading about positionality, I thought researchers needed to go a bit deeper into that connection between narrative and personal story.

I had many aspects of my personal identity that were at work in my thoughts and teaching, and working with teachers, as well as how people see me. With a feminist lens around my work, I thought something was missing. Yes, gender is important, but there are many other aspects of my identity also working together to help me think deeper about my experiences so that I could also understand the experiences of teachers I was working with. How can I talk about my identities collectively because it's not really easy to separate them out? Positional identities have to do with the intersectionality of multiple social markers that shape how we see ourselves, and specifically how we see ourselves as teachers, while also engaging with how Self shapes how we teach and how we develop relationships with students, and with science. This guided my dissertation work and work as a faculty member.

Relatively recently, I would say about five years ago, I started reading critical race theory. I began reading law articles and books to understand the early movement of critical legal studies to help me understand critical race theory and critical race theory in education. I was hesitant to do a racial framing because I see my multiple identities. But I started by reading Crenshaw and Harris and reading the early work of intersectionality. I started reading another book that gave a historical account of intersectionality even before Crenshaw, and I thought, 'Now I get it.' Critical race theory and intersectionality added to positional identity a deeper way for me to understand and talk about the importance of race with other social markers. I then developed a course in teacher education for doctoral students to make connections of theory and practice with race in teacher education focused on developing teacher educators.

When I go back and look at my work from the past, and even now, it has always had a leaning towards critical race theory and intersectionality. I've taken up critical race theory but really looking at intersectionality and disciplinary connections related to science teacher education. To me, it's really the marriage where positionality and intersectionality come together because intersectionality foregrounds experiences of Black women as being very different than Black males, and very different from White women, so I was like, 'Finally!' In turn, I am now understanding the racial and gender pieces much more than in my previous work.

Oftentimes in identity frameworks, they talk about how you see yourself and how other people see you. This is tricky. People do not always see you as you see yourself. Then, how do you position yourself to be seen and, even if no one recognizes you, don't you still see yourself?

I'm still foregrounding how I see myself and looking at positionality in terms of thinking of how I position myself in the world as an African American woman from the south – you know, all of that – how I position myself first and then how do other people see me.

But I think in other frameworks of identity, you can't have your identity because it is how other people are seeing you. But who cares how other people see you? That's also part of exclusion. Why would I exclude parts of me? For example, I see me in this particular way. Other people may not see me in that particular way, so does that make my perspectives that I share from my vantage point not as relevant or strong? We cannot lose that sense of agency about ourselves because we are so concerned about how other people are seeing us. This occurs in science: 'Who is a scientist or who gets to be a scientist?' If I waited for someone to call me a scientist, I would never be a scientist based upon my narrative. We have to be able to look at identity in how we position our Self in the world. To me, that's where positional identities are really grounded – first in the person and, second, in how other people are seeing you.

PB: I think this really transitions well into thinking about the readers themselves. Often these books are taken up by teachers in methods courses and they are probably thinking, 'Why am I required to read these types of perspectives on exclusion and its connection to narrative?' What advice would you give to them in terms of the importance of learning these ideas?

FM: First of all, because I'm still very much grounded in the Self, teachers need to read this book so they can learn more about who they are and learn about themselves – unpacking their positions. As they learn about themselves, they can start to say, 'Okay, how do my perspectives more or less compare to someone else's perspective – where do I fit myself into how other people are thinking'? Not necessarily to grade yourself, but to say, especially with this particular book, 'Am I being exclusive? Am I being inclusive? What are the ways I can start to not leave out aspects of myself and my students, or what are the ways I am excluding others?' You have to deal with yourself and get to know yourself at a deeper level.

Therefore, as teachers read the different chapters in this book, some of the things might not apply to them, some positional markers may not apply to you, but it does not mean that you can exclude yourself from reflecting and questioning your narrative vis-à-vis how the authors of the different chapters, the students, and the curriculum examples shared in the chapters are being presented. As teachers start to understand their personal Self, then they start to figure out, 'How might I understand my *students* better?' This book offers insights about how or what your students may be going through, as well as how teachers can support them. Even though the readers may not be able to put themselves directly in the authors' shoes, they can be more human, caring, and loving. You know, I can't be you. I don't have the same experiences you have, Phillip, but I know from my own personal narrative and the things that excluded me, I can understand your experiences and narratives.

I was telling someone recently, we don't teach empathy and sometimes we think empathy is such a bad word, it's not a bad word. It helps you to better understand somebody else's life, their experiences. It involves emotion, all of that, and we don't teach that very well, which we very much need today. And then what do you do with all of that, how do you really act upon the inequities and disparities and everything that's going on in schools and society? But you can't do any action if you have not taken the time to understand your own personal story and try to find ways to connect it with somebody else's.

PB: That makes a lot of sense and I completely agree with you, especially being a former teacher. I was actually in an elementary classroom today talking to a teacher about how her interactions with her students were probably not as explicit as she wanted them to be and the students were responding in kind. They were set up to say, 'I don't really know your expectations so I'm going to be me,' and that comes with all the differential positions that the students come into the classroom with so you're not going to expect the same response. This alludes to this final question, and I really want to give you the last word to speak on this: The readers of the book are likley to come from a lot of different positions, such as researchers, teachers, policymakers, but we always sort of look back and say, 'Oh, I wish I would've known that, then.' So what do you have to say to readers before they start to read – what do you wish someone had told you years ago when you started your journey towards adopting a critical consciousness in education and working toward equity?

FM: You know, I thought it was going to be easier than it is. I thought that once you told people and they see these inequities they would be like, 'Oh, let's change,' but it doesn't happen that quickly. I have found over the years, now I'm telling my doctoral students and younger teachers who are anxious and excited for change, 'No, it's not going to happen overnight. It might not even happen next semester.' But then say, 'don't stop, because you never know when it's going to happen.'

As a teacher, in terms of the students I would have in my classroom, you have no idea what their life is going to be like. But you pour into them and you give whatever you can for that academic year or semester that you have them, and you pray and hope everything will go well with their lives. I had to understand that as a teacher, I won't really know what's going to happen to everybody, unless a student happens to come back and tells me what's going on with them. Part of the life of a teacher is that you just have to make sure that you've given all that you can give in that moment that you are entrusted with them. Pray that life will treat them as you would've treated them. It circles around and around. I wish people had told me more around that you just have to trust that you're doing good work and that if they never come back and tell you, you have to say within yourself, 'I did do good,' or you have to say, 'I really didn't do such a good job; let me be better for the next group.' Just continue that way.

I've always been a reflective person, wanting to always do better and always do good, and so if people don't have that kind of reflective practice about themselves, that's what I would tell them: Really be reflective about what you've done and what you contributed and try to do better all the time. You may never perfect it, you can't perfect it, but you can move toward perfection by improving your practice daily as you go on.

Again, I wish someone would have told me that it was going to be tougher than I thought it was going to be, or I wish they would've told me don't assume that once you've told people to 'do the right thing' that they would do it. I had to learn people are not going to do what you want them to do. You do what you can do.

Chapter 1

ADOPTING ANOTHER POINT OF VIEW ON HOPE

Intersectional Equity from the Margins

CARLOS ADAMS

Some misunderstood and undervalued aspects of exclusionary practices are the relationships among hope, power, and exclusion. The process of exclusion and the individuals and collectives involved in this process maintain a relationship to hope. One side hopes to break free from the bonds of exclusion, and another side hopes to strengthen those bonds, yet little has been written about hope's relationship to power and exclusion. What does it mean to hope? How can two opposing sides hope to escape the bonds or hope to strengthen the bonds simultaneously? Which side utilizes hope towards something positive and which side manipulates hope for something negative? How important is it to understand the function of hope and how hope functions? Finally, what is the relationship among hope, power and exclusion? These are just a few of the questions I wondered about, which kept me awake at night, searching for something that might help explain my lived experiences and those around me.

Exclusion develops from who has access to power and those who do not. It is about the acquisition and maintenance of power. Exclusion is about how a society defines and implements power and is intimately connected to who is considered expendable and who is not. An individual, collective, system, or institution cannot exclude without power and while there may be an ability to separate, to distinguish, and to create divisions without power, these actions lack the ability to maintain these separations, differences, and divisions. Exclusionary practices are about how a society values and interacts with differences – perceived or real. As I look back at my life experiences, I find this narrative of power working to exclude in

P.A. Boda (ed.), Essays on Exclusion, 21–37.

ways that are both overt and covert, which required me to think from another point of view, a new way of making sense:

> At college, I felt like an outsider, venturing into unwelcoming and possibly hostile spaces. A college education was never considered important for someone like me: Brown and working class. College was for the White and wealthy. My family saw working with my hands as inevitable, and the schools saw working with my hands as my destiny. No one ever mentioned college as an option in my life. I had no choice but to believe them for so many years. I eventually dropped out of high school and sought inclusion through drugs.

My narrative frames exclusion to mean more than denying or inhibiting access to economic, educational, and social resources. Exclusion, then, involves all material and non-material aspects of culture and society: hegemonic influences, ideologies, aesthetics, rhetorical strategies, discursive paradigms, and cultural artifacts. All of which involve the dualistic constructions of centers and margins, self and other, normal or deviant. Given this reality, exclusion operates in a way that ensures its dynamic ability to reduce complexities into a singular and verifiable differences in order to deny any similarities among the parties involved – this becomes the underlying justification for exclusion and inclusion (Memmi, 2006). It is in this way that exclusion should be viewed and deconstructed in our attempts to build new modes of interaction leading to equity; this is where I believe we should start, and what this chapter provides to the conversation about equity and exclusion in education.

On Intersectionality and Exclusion: My Position

Exclusion takes on a variety of locations and each carries its own significance in relation to how power operates within it. Taking an intersectional view towards power and positioning (Crenshaw, 1991), thus, complicates exclusion by allowing the possibilities of inhabiting multiple points of inclusion and exclusion simultaneously – by illuminating how one understands the ways in which individuals negotiate these various inclusive and exclusive positions. Intersectionality also allows for understanding how each attribute, such as race and gender, are associated with systemic and institutional power with an understanding that not all systemic and institutional powers has the same impact. This also emphasizes that contexts produce particular consequences that differ by demographic and that by understanding how different aspects of systemic and institutional power access different degrees of power, exclusion can be seen in a more fluid state and measured in diverse ways than it has been to determine the extent of exclusion and the ability to negate exclusion in the moments that it shows its ugly head. For example, as a man I know I am not excluded from the benefits of patriarchy but as a working-class Brown man, I don't benefit from patriarchy in the same ways a wealthy White man does in the United States of America. This, again, comes from my own lived experiences and, therefore, provides an epistemological position from which to engage with exclusion in ways that are not always taken up by equity. To illuminate this point, in the excerpt below, I reflect on the nature of power and structure as they influence my hopes, goals, and dreams, while also revealing the need for hope:

> The exclusion I felt and still feel in education reminds me of my inability to imagine more than I dare, power denies me the ability to realize the resources and tools by locking them inside of a bureaucracy and renders any actualization to fleeting moments existing only in my classroom. In the end, this may be all there is and maybe, just maybe, it is enough: For now.

As I move into a discussion on hope, let me acknowledge how I realize I am on shaky ground. My insecurities have me doubt if my ideas on hope are legitimate or just ramblings of a person unsure of his potential. My ideas about hope stem from the research I did for my dissertation: *Machismo and Geographies of Hope* (Adams, 2014). I am still not sure if I understand the function of hope, but I am sure there is a lack of discussion concerning hope in relation to equity in education. This stems from, I feel, a simple misunderstanding that hope is universal. We all hope and, therefore, assume access to hope operates in the same way. This universal assumption – this inherent misunderstanding of hope – prevents our ability to complicate and contextualize the nature of hope: i.e., to determine the ways in which an individual or collective access and utilizes hope to provide the strength and energy to the collective, which allows hope to flourish. It is my goal to parse out the nuanced nature of hope in relation to more intersectional analyses so that exclusion, and by proxy distortions of power, can be more holistically understood.

Intersectional Hope

My ideas and investigations into the function of hope began when reading Paulo Freire's insightful book, *The Pedagogy of Hope* (1994). Throughout the book, Freire brings in examples of hope but never truly defines what hope is, which led me to ask myself what my definition of hope is – interestingly, I found I lacked one. I assumed it was a feeling of some sort that helped an individual achieve a goal. I began to ask others around me what their definition was and found many did not have one either, nor had they took the time to seriously think of one. In the end, everyone I talked to defined hope as something positive leading to something better.

Yet, I thought Hitler had hope, didn't he? How and why was his hope so very different from the hope my friends and I described to each other? In what ways does hope operate differentially among different groups of people embracing hope in the world? I concluded hope is truly democratic in that if everyone does not have access to the function of hope and, more importantly, does not have access to the ways in which hope functions in the same way, or to the same extent, then hope is being manipulated to serve the needs of those in power – a ruling elite – and it becomes hijacked by the power that people embody, adopt, and exude when hope actualizes into reality. Hitler's relationship to hope denied this access to over six million individuals and this denial constitutes a distortion of hope, not a representation of hope in its democratic form.

This recognition also made me realize how hope, which is something so crucial to everyone in their day-to-day lives, had been so poorly understood by not only scholars but also the general populous. No one could easily define hope beyond some universal feeling, which meant hope's function, and how hope functions, would go undiscovered given that our own nuanced understandings of this idea had yet to be deconstructed and interrogated. I began to research hope and found little in terms of how hope related to peoples' everyday lives; I found most of the research about hope was connected to healing, physical and mental, or theological – how hope relates to peoples' everlasting and spiritual needs.

My research led me to define the function of hope as a mechanism that initiates, propels, and sustains an individual or collective towards something deemed significant to them, and not necessarily an idea that will have a positive effect on all peoples. I define hope as a mechanism – an entity leading to a process – because hope is more than a feeling involved in physical and psychological healing, or a faith-based longing. Like other mechanisms, hope serves a particular function and, therein, functions in particular ways based on the contexts in which it is used and the characters enacting it. I discovered hope functions through three distinct geographies: imagination, realization, and actualization. Through this view, hope becomes just as, if not more, salient in the discussion on exclusion in education, and helps up bring out new points of view on how to achieve more equitable practices overall. In turn, an interrogation of hope starts to unpack for us questions such as, whose hope is valued, and when? As well as, when does someone's hopes become devalued, and why?

Exclusion and Its Connection to Hope

When addressing exclusion and exclusionary practices, one element generally missing, but vital, is hope in relation to the definition I described previously. Those that are excluded fight to end their exclusion and, in doing so, hope becomes a force for change both in their own psyches and in their collective consciousness. When a dominant group fights to maintain exclusion, hope becomes a force for domination in that each group attempts to access hope, yet with different goals: oppression or liberation – each group 'hopes' they will survive and thrive this conflictual experience, but for very different purposes and drawing on very different justifications for their hope. So, how does hope relate to each group's activities and ideologies? Moreover, if hope is involved in both endeavors then the nature of hope needs to be part of the discussion of how to address exclusion that is produced from the hopes and goals of the parties involved, without which the nature of exclusion is not thoroughly engaged in a holistic and intersectional sense because the contexts that have led up to these hopes being part of these particular parties' ideas are not interrogated for their contributions to this confrontation.

Yet, this vital force for change is rarely defined and described and, given this reality, I argue hope needs to be addressed as being grounded in the material world and, as such, not everyone can access hope in the same way because of the material realities that are produced by the nature of how power operates to divide and exclude. Given how exclusionary practices prevent or inhibit some from accessing hope in the same way as those in the dominant group access hope, the denial of access is directly related to one's own ability to access hope in particular contexts and histories, as well as what type of power such a person holds when set in juxtaposition to those who embody the privileged – the powerful ruling elite; or, in simpler terms, those that are not negatively affected by exclusionary ideas and practices. This becomes paramount when thinking about exclusion in education, which is highlighted in the excerpt below where I have found hope interweaving with power and privilege:

> I am, at the time of this writing, an adjunct professor, meaning I have less access to power than almost anyone else on campus. I've been passed over for a tenure-track position more times than I can remember. My hope was to reach a position where I felt some sense of security lacking throughout

my life. What I realized was how those with power are the gatekeepers, making sure the person hired meets the job announcement's minimum requirements and, more importantly, meets the needs of the division to hire those who go along to get along.

I interviewed for a new tenure-track position for a set of American Minority and Ethnic Studies courses at the community college I worked at for several years. Except for one year, I was the only one teaching these classes. When I walked into the interview, I saw the committee comprised of four White professors and administrators and one Black professor. None of them had taught in an ethnic studies division or program and two, I believe, had never taught an ethnic studies class.

Needless to say, I didn't get the position. The power of the committee had chosen a younger White woman with less than one year of experience teaching ethnic studies classes compared to my over-twenty years of experience. There's no way of knowing whether it was liberal White supremacy or ageism or a combination of the two that prevented me from actualizing my hope for stability. Yet, my experience explains the intersectionality of hope when it comes to exclusion and inclusion.

The ability to include and exclude, thus, also involves the way hope functions in society more broadly because of its connection to societal positions of power. Whether or not the issue is about inclusion or exclusion, hope becomes an aspect of either one given its interconnection to power, and therein exclusion. Whether inclusion works counter-intuitively to maintain dominance and regulate the allotment of resources, or exclusion works in similar ways to eliminate the dominance and democratize the allotment of resources, hope is always involved. The pragmatic act of exclusion directly impacts people's abilities to hope; it defines what it is they can or should hope for (as seen in my first excerpt in this chapter), and how people can actualize their goals, which derives their purpose from people's hopes.

One interesting thing about exclusion is how often we let the tactics meant to marginalize us lead us to believe we deserve such alienation. Is it not hope that allows us to see how alienation can be overcome and why it needs to be overcome? The ability to imagine, realize, and actualize isn't something always recognizable nor is it necessarily vocalized and we don't understand how we have dealt with the exclusion until it's gone – until the exclusive practices have made their mark on the person, forever scarring them and positioning them, more often than not, as 'less-than' those that have been included. Here is where the significance of hope becomes apparent, both theoretically and pragmatically.

Hope generally relates to two aspects of life: the act of acquiring – related to the material – and the act of becoming – concerning the personal. When it comes to issues of exclusion, hope can also be both at the same time. Acquiring involves obtaining the material goods within a society, and the personal involves a person's or collective's growth and enrichment – their perceived worth. The distribution of wealth, material goods and resources away from the masses and towards the growing economically and socially elite denies a fair allocation of wealth, material goods, and resources for all. Thus, the self-loathing and self-hatred associated with this type of exclusion inhibits personal growth, as well as stifles hope from empowering people being excluded to dream of more. If not inhibiting, then it definitely delays growth and enrichment – at least in my case. Was it not for such exclusion, maybe the nature and actualization of my hope would have helped sustain different goals for myself, as well as others, highlighted below in an excerpt from a dialogue with my mother about my past experiences with hope, exclusion, and power:

> 'If it wasn't for your stepfather, you wouldn't be the man you are today,' my mother said one night when we were talking about the abuse I suffered from my White stepfather. He was a mean man and even meaner when he was drunk. He never accomplished what he wanted in his life and never tried to be a better man. He shared whatever pain he was going through with his family. If he hurt, then we would hurt. I don't know if it was because I was the oldest or because I was the darkest, but it seemed to me I became the one he would share his pain with the most. I replied to my mother, 'Don't give me that whatever doesn't kill you, makes you stronger, Nietzschean crap. I would have been the man I am today 25 years ago had it not been for him. It's taken me that long to come to terms with what he did. It's taken me that long to believe I deserved better and could be better.'

It's taken me that long to hope...

As described earlier, the function of hope acts as a mechanism that initiates, sustains, and propels an individual or collective towards something deemed significant. As a mechanism, hope, therefore, functions in certain ways. I discovered three ways hope functions in a society: imagination, realization, and actualization. Imagination is the creative force needed to envision the something deemed significant. Realization is when the individual or collective realizes and gains access to the necessary resources and tools needed to achieve the something deemed significant. Actualization is when the something deemed significant is achieved. The abuse I suffered from my White stepfather reduced what I could imagine, disguised many of the available resources and tools, and rendered any actualization of any of my goals to something I was unworthy of.

Though each one of these functions act independently, they also act in conjunction with one another. The ways hope functions derive from the interaction among the three factors. There are those times when what the imagination envisions changes because access to the tools and resources warrant or compel changes, and therein the inevitable actualization takes on a different significance and meaning.

I never realized the extent of exclusion, particularly through ageism, present in higher education until I reached the age when exclusion from certain academic positions becomes the norm rather than the exception. Few on the campuses I worked at really wanted to talk about it, as though talking about it would trigger a sense of apprehension stemming from the idea that good people could never exclude due to age. For me, this ageism became apparent when I noticed how colleges and universities rarely hired anyone over the age of fifty for tenure-track positions. I know of two from the hundreds of such hires. Many of my fellow adjuncts over the age of 50 understand how excluded we are from consideration for tenure-track positions. Many, like me, gave up on the goal of tenured. Instead, we hope for something different: teach enough classes per semester or quarter to thrive instead of simply survive, to retire with some dignity, and to appreciate when the act of teaching and learning becomes liberatory.

The Intersections of Imagination

Imagination provides the impetus to discover a different view of what the material world can become. It is ancestral, historical, relevant, and inventive. It inspires individuals and collectives to seek something more than they have or are now. Imagination transcends social limitations and provides possibilities of new and creative futures. Imagination embraces all that we are – not just who we think we are. Imagination weaves the material, spiritual, and lived experiences into both an ethereal dream and a goal to be actualized. It is unpredictable and, at times, alarming. Most importantly of all, imagination is, as is hope, grounded in the material world, while fantasy often pursues creative thought outside or beyond the material world. The imagination used to envision something deemed significant must also be grounded in the material world because of their inextricable connections – we imagine changes in either the personal or material realms as a process of actualizing hope.

Exclusion, however, works to limit the imagination, thus inhibiting hope from ever aiding in the growth of our society, as well as ourselves. In this way, exclusion seeks to maintain a sense of control over the imagination and often takes the form of imagining only what the ruling elites can use to their advantage – i.e., exclusion designs the imagination of those living in deficit ideologies of oppression rather than fostering new ways of looking at their lived realities. If what is imagined disrupts the power of a dominant group, then the dominant group seeks to co-opt the vision.

These exclusive uses of hope and power can be seen throughout modern-day musical traditions that were once used for uplifting marginalized populations but become commodified (e.g., hip-hop and corridos) and stems from the fundamental need for those in power to sustain power through the inhibition of hope being disseminated to the masses. If those in power can't co-opt it, then they try to invalidate it – this drawing back to the example of hip-hop wherein one example of commodified rap is then generalized as the deficit narrative of all those who listen to it, or those it was supposedly 'designed for' (i.e., people of color). If they can't invalidate, then they try to marginalize it in ways where it is cast away from any narrative and positioned as not worthy of any attention. If they can't marginalize it, then they seek to silence it. And finally, if they can't silence it, then they eliminate it. This trope has been seen throughout history within the colonialization process and the nature of representation, but has connections with hope, exclusion, and power.

Exclusion uses 'divide and conquer' techniques to limit the ways in which imagination can unify and seeks to get each excluded individual or collective to imagine only the something that serves dominating needs and desires, even if is at the cost of another excluded group. This designed vision disproportionately divides resources and tools from becoming accessible to one group and invests more to another, pitting the groups in competition against one another for the available resources, instead of directing the energy towards the derivation of this disparity: exclusion. In this way, the imagining process of hope is stifled and siloed into pockets of possibility where some can envision new futures but only enough to suffice the narrative of hope being imposed onto them – never imagining a material reality beyond that which was designed for those deemed as not deserving of creating their own reality. This is why we need to break down how hope operates and view it through different perspectives: most importantly, to define and deconstruct old narratives of self and society, starting the process of creating new interpretations of self and society.

The Intersections of Realization

Realization is when an individual or collective begins to identify and utilize the necessary tools and resources it takes to actualize the something deemed significant. This entails the development of skills: physical, written, and verbal. The physical pertains to the body given that an individual or collective must learn to use the body as a source of reclamation: reclaiming the body from its colonial prison, healing the colonial scars. The written includes both the ability to read and the ability to write. Reading desires something more than simply looking at the message, it requires the understanding of motive, the appreciation of truth, the recognition of location, and the intuitiveness of thinking. Along similar lines, the written demands more than simply applying words: It demands the courage to transgress, the ability to transcend, the righteousness of honesty.

Finally, the verbal involves the development of listening and speaking skills. In my dissertation I looked only at verbal and rhetorical skills. I add listening skills because the act of listening, rather than just hearing, is revolutionary. These skills involve eliminating distractions, reacting to intonation, initiating an internal conversation, and discovering hidden meanings. Through these three skills, realization also involves acquiring material resources. Economic power cannot be undervalued because it is often at the heart of exclusion and without the redistribution of wealth – of capital: material, psychological, and spiritual – those that seek new narratives can only imagine these resources through colonial logics, those same logics used to devalue them in the first place and deny them hope.

A key aspect involved in the development of the skills needed to access tools and resources involves what Patrick Shade calls "Habits of Hope." For Shade (2001), in order for hope to move from a spontaneous moment of imagination into the geography of realization, individuals or collectives need to nurture habits of hope because habits of hope, in terms of negotiating the geographies of realization, take on two key approaches: passive and active. In their passive state, habits of hope develop a sense of acquiescence where the individual or collective allows those with greater access to hegemonic power to manipulate the imagination, disguise the tools and resources, and render actualization to what benefits those in control. Furthermore, in its passive state, habits of hope become co-opted. The passive state of hope requires little attention, resists scrutiny and silences critiques. In their active state, habits of hope provide the necessary motivation and consciousness needed to question the formation of centers and margins thereby determining the range of options available to subvert centers and reinforce margins. The active state of hope requires vigorous attention, constant scrutiny, and remains vulnerable to critique – it is active in all senses of the word.

In my classes, I utilize a short story by Toni Morrison (1992) entitled "Racitatif" to demonstrate the problems associated with colorblindness, which is the younger generation's dominant racial ideology. The story revolves around several meetings between the two protagonists: Twyla and Roberta. In each meeting, Morrison uses stereotypes to explore each character's agency. I ask the students to choose one of the characters and which race the character is associated with and provide one example to support their answer. If they are unsure who is White or Black, then I have them write down unsure and give one example as to why they are unsure. After they are done, I let them know that they all see race because Morrison never tells us the race of either main character. I also let them know that they see race through stereotypes because, for most of them, it is the stereotypes that they have the most experience.

I make it clear no one can leave the classroom after this exercise claiming they are colorblind. At this moment, I raise two key questions: first, why is race the only aspect of an individual or collective identity they want to erase? And, second, what is it about race that frightens or threatens us so much that they want to eliminate race? They are not talking about erasing gender, sexuality, class status, disability etc. – only race. I let them know how they are also talking about gender and sexuality, as well as many other issues of identity, more than at any time in U.S. history, as well as class status more since the great depression.

Their inability to answer either of these questions, with any certainty, relates to the passive and active aspects of the habits of hope. Many of them have passively accepted colorblindness as a way to end racism: race isn't an issue unless one makes it an issue. They hope by ignoring race, it will simply vanish. Many passively believe they can deal with racial differences by simply hoping the differences no longer exist. Active involvement with hope requires much more. I believe this active status of hope manifests itself through Paulo Freire's idea on what he calls conscientização: critical consciousness. In terms of hope, conscientização imagines new and creative futures, explores the terrains where tools and resources reside, and critiques the availability and construction of various tools and resources that compel individuals or collectives towards the something deemed democratically significant.

While discussing the problems associated with colorblindness, students begin to envision a new significance. While the goal of ending racism remains, their imagination envisions the possibility that maybe erasing race is not the answer. They begin to wonder if the issue is about how society can recognize the significance of race while eliminating the value placed on race. I explain to them that, from my perspective, what I hear so many of them is about being *value-blind*, not colorblind. Next, they remain open to the idea that the path to ending the value placed on race travels through race, not sidestepping race as colorblindness dictates. At this moment, students can now discover the tools and resources available, enabling them to actualize their vision.

They now experience hope in its active state.

The Intersections of Actualization

The final aspect of the ways hope functions is actualization. Actualization occurs when the individual or collective obtains the something deemed significant. Whatever the imagination envisions and whatever resources and tools were utilized arrive at the moment when the significant something becomes real in the life or lives of the individual or collective. Actualization is seen as the culmination of the intersections between imagination and realization. A sense of accomplishment filters through the individual or collective as hope becomes a reality.

Actualization relates to the two other key significant aspects of hope I mentioned previously. The first way actualization relates involves the act of becoming: the growth of an individual or collective deemed desirable. As human beings, we are always involved in the act of becoming – it's the fluid social nature of evolution. Hope connects to this process of becoming; the imagination envisioned what it is an individual or collective want to become, and realization provides the necessary tools and resources indispensable to growth. The second way involves the act of acquiring the material goods and services needed to survive and thrive.

The food we eat, the shelters we live within, the commodities we accumulate, reside within the act of acquiring. Unlike the act of becoming, the act of acquiring has a material existence. Whether actualization pertains to the act of becoming (where a person or collective experience actually changes in thought or behavior) or pertains to the act of acquiring (where the object no longer remains elusive and can be touched, seen, smelled, or heard) suggests actualization necessitates finality. More importantly, actualization is seen as permanent, resulting from the end of a process. The process reaches a culmination; there's nothing more.

However, I believe actualization lacks permanence. Whether it is about the act of becoming or the act of acquiring, nothing the imagination envisions is absolute. Any actualization of becoming involves a continuing process of growth, ending only on the day we pass away. In the act of acquiring, anything material has a finite life span. Its usefulness ultimately ceases. In this way, the imagination always looks for something beyond the life span of a material object. We are in a constant search of replacing that which has outlived its usefulness (Shade, 2001). This impermanence plays an important role for the excluded among us. The idea of change becomes something that is not a result but a continuing process to include/exclude.

This impermanence demands an awareness to see how change is generational. The nature of the struggle and the discursive strategies within the struggle should be defined by each succeeding generation. The imagination needs to be allowed the ability to explore new and creative futures, each generation must be allowed to define the necessary tools and develop the indispensable resources – each generation must come to terms with the impermanence of hope in their own way. The universal aspect of hope prevents further exploration of the ways in which hope generates new and creative futures. Those in control rely on the myth that since we all hope, we all hope in the same way. This inhibits agency among the excluded and can lead to a sense of fatalism.

At the end of the quarter, many students want solutions they can implement. "You've shown us all this crap about oppressing people but no solutions," they cry out. I reply, "This isn't a math test. The solutions need to be contextual depending on the historical moment." I continue by stating, "You students are in a unique moment in your lives. It is while at college where you can learn to fight the good fight, make mistakes and not be fired." As educators, I feel it is up to us to promote civic engagement by helping students learn about how to hold people with power accountable for the things they say or don't say, as well as the things they do or don't do, even if it means the students' engagement is directed at me. In addition, I let them talk about their role in the third and final racial civil rights movement: the first being the abolition of slavery, the second being the abolition of Jim Crow, and the third is the elimination of the master/servant consciousness that is key to maintaining White supremacy.

Hope's actualization, as impermanent and contextual, allows for hope to adjust in order to meet the needs of each new generation. Hope makes what was once invisible to one generation visible to another generation, while remaining flexible enough to suit the nature of each generational discourse and the relationships each group has to power. Understanding and accepting the impermanence of actualization provide hope with the newfound energy needed to revive hope for each subsequent generation.

We must also be aware of how the acts of becoming and acquiring easily slip into a process of commodification. We begin to turn all aspects of life into acquired commodities. We often fall victim to turning everything into something that has a monetary value, including hope. If hope lacks economic value, then we may dismiss it as useless or, worse, distort the usefulness of hope only for economic wealth and individual self-interest. We turn on each other thinking this betrayal serves a purpose. We can excuse our behavior by blaming the system that causes the problems, not the individuals or collectives that benefit from this structured and designed system of exclusion. This is a struggle within excluded communities. When dominant society glorifies commodities as the something worth hoping for, the excluded can fall victim to being absorbed into the center of oppression rather than utilize the power found in the margins to enact change and disrupt the oppressive structures found in the centers of a society – those delineated with value.

With this in mind, maybe the idea is to not hope for inclusion into the centers. Maybe hope should be framed as the dissolution of the centers in order for those in the center to move into the margins where new and creative futures reside (hooks, 1984). Centers are usually anti-evolutionary. What was true in the past is true today and will be true in the future. Centers deny the ability to allow for the evolution of human understanding. Margins are dynamic, constantly shifting and constantly evolving. They allow for possibilities to become realities. Margins create an environment where exclusionary tactics and the designating of difference lack the power to enforce rigidity. While centers reinforce existing definitions and uses power in order to maintain that rigidity, margins reflect fluidity that redefines power from something used to dominate or compete with that power to uses for true cooperation (Anzaldúa, 1987).

I was introduced to Gloria Anzaldúa in 1993 during my 2nd year of college. As with most, she confused and enlightened me at the same time. Her ideas on borderland identity seemed to provide me with an understanding of my multiracial identity. Her ideas on fluid, rather than dualistic, thinking were something I searched for during my adult life. I thought I understood why eliminating dualistic thinking would end the violence in my life. I made this a key part of the commencement speech I gave when I graduated from Western Washington University. It wasn't until a few years later when I began to truly understand what she meant. She addressed issues of identity but also power. In order for power to be defined and used for domination or competition, power needs to have a solid foundational structure so power can dig its roots into and entrench itself in a society. Dualistic Thinking provides the perfect foundation for power to dominate, to exist. If a mass revolutionary change from dualistic to fluid perceptions of identity, ideology, systems, and institution can occur, then power lacks the solid foundation needed to be oppressive. Every time power attempts to dig its roots into a solid foundation, the foundation shifts and power loses its ability to oppress.

In terms of the act of becoming, the actualization of growth and personal enrichment often can be sidetracked and disguised to look like it's what the imagination envisions when it is what the dominant group allows to be envisioned. I realized this at work in higher education. The halls of academia become sites best described as white-collar vocational-technical institutes. Most of my students do not enroll into my classes in ethnic studies because they want to engage with the act of becoming. Most don't even know what ethnic studies means. They enroll because it becomes an act of acquiring: It meets a requirement. Their goal is not to gain knowledge to develop a deeper understanding of the world and their place in it. Their hope is reduced to understanding that unless the knowledge leads to economic profit, it serves little purpose. They are there to get white-collar jobs so they don't have to sweat for a living: to buy the granite countertops, the house with the two-car garage, and the trips to Disneyland. Their imagination is reduced to the act of acquiring, they only seek the necessary tools and resources needed to acquire, and the something they acquire must have a monetary value. The significance of the act of becoming remains elusive, lost in a space where economic success means one is only a better person when one is successful in a capitalist economic system: The more the economic success, the better the person. Successful people become the role models; their needs and desires become integrated into excluded individuals' needs and desires.

Conclusive Remarks

I wrote my dissertation on the attempts by Chicanos and Latinos to redefine their masculinity called Machismo. They sought to become a better man. Yet, in every case, the writers just didn't get it, according to many Chicana feminist writers. Their adherence to patriarchy formed the foundation of their words and studies. I wonder if the problem wasn't an inability to move beyond the influence of patriarchy and misogyny, but a misunderstanding of the hope embedded in attempting to redefine machismo in order to develop new and creative futures with the women in their/mine lives/life, so I decided to investigate hope.

I developed my own theory on the function of hope and how hope functions and apply it to the writings of Chicanos/Latinos about their masculinity. The goal was to allow my ideas on hope to act as a red flag when describing machismo. If Chicanos and Latinos just didn't get it, even when incorporating various gender and social theories, then maybe my ideas on hope could serve as a way to distinguish between the negative and positive ideas in our writings. Maybe hope could be more than a force or inspiration or mechanism; maybe hope could be a way to determine what change is needed and how that change should inform men's relationship to Machismo, and other forms of toxic masculinity emboldened in almost all aspects of the fabric of our societies. If in our words, thoughts, and actions a structure remains in place that denies some greater access to the ways hope functions, and denies or inhibits access to the ways hope functions, then maybe hope can expose that exclusion and, in doing so, allow for people to change their words, thoughts, and actions so the democratic aspect of hope prevails in a society.

Implications

To understand intersectional hope means to eliminate the idea of a universal hope. While the function of hope may be able to transcend cultural and societal borders in that hope's function, as a mechanism, initiates, sustains, and propels an individual or collective towards something deemed significant, the way hope performs this function deserves a deeper conversation into the nature of hope that is currently being had in scholarship. While it may be true that we all hope, I argue what isn't true is that we all hope in the same way. Hope resides within the material and non-material world and, as such, is impacted by the material world and the ideologies that form the basis of a given society.

What a better understanding of intersectional hope allows for is a deeper discussion into how hope functions in any given society. The three geographies of hope I've identified so far (imagination, realization, and actualization) provide a way to deconstruct the ideologies and the material world each function resides in. A deeper understanding explores who has access to these three geographies and who does not, as well as how does an individual or collective gain access to any of these geographies. A deeper understanding allows for an uncovering of the ways in which these three functions intersect with each other and opens up possibilities to use these three geographies to determine if hope is truly democratic or if hope is being manipulated to serve the needs of ruling elites.

My ideas on the function of hope and the ways in which hope performs this function is in its infancy. My goal, or better yet, *my hope* is to further the conversation about hope. If hope is a part of our everyday lives, yet few can adequately define hope, let alone describe how hope functions in a society, this allows hope to be manipulated. This lack of dialogue on hope means exclusion remains intact and the ability to eliminate the structures of exclusion remains distant – forever out of reach of those that are exclude and, therein, need to access it the most.

I am now near the age of retirement. I've suffered the indignities of exclusion my whole life. Sometimes I wonder what life would look or feel like without the indignities. Would I feel as though something was missing? Would inclusion seem so unfamiliar if I lacked the skills needed to negotiate this unfamiliar terrain? It is through the intersectionality of hope that keeps me moving forward. I see the obstacles that lie before me and understand some can be overcome and others cannot. I no longer strive to overcome insurmountable barriers; I am too old to have the time it takes to overcome these barriers. I channel my imagination towards those things deemed significant that can be actualized in my life. I access the resources in ways that allow for others to join me, and I actualize those things that are a priority. I awake each day exploring the prospect of possibilities available to me. For isn't this the essence of intersectional hope: The prospect of possibilities?

REFERENCES

Adams, C. (2014). *Machismo and Geographies of Hope*. Riga, Latvia: Lambert Academic Publishing.

Anzaldúa, G. (1987) *Borderlands/La Frontera: The New Mestiza*. San Francisco: Aunt Lute Book Company.

Crenshaw, K. (1991). Mapping the margins: Intersectionality, identity politics, and violence against women of color. *Stanford Law Review*, 1241-1299.

Freire, P. (1994). *Pedagogy of hope* (RR Barr, Trans.). New York: Continuum.

hooks, b (1984) *Feminist theory: From margin to center*. New York: Routledge.

Memmi, A. (2005). "Assigning value to difference". In P. Rothenberg (Ed.), *Beyond borders: Thinking critically about global issues* (p. 173-179). New York: Worth Publishers.

Morrison, T. (1992). "Recitatif". In I. Reed, K. Trueblood, & S. Wong (Eds.), *The before Columbus foundation fiction anthology*. New York: W.W. Norton and Company.

Shade, P. (2001). *Habits of hope: A pragmatic theory*. Nashville: Vanderbilt University Press.

Chapter 2

EXCLUDED FROM THE BEGINNING

Black, Female, and Born in the Bronx

YOLANDA SEALEY-RUIZ

In his 2016 book, *Stamped from the Beginning: The Definitive History of Racist Ideas in America*, Ibram X. Kendi makes a compelling argument that racist ideas did not arise from ignorance and the hatred of Blacks, but from a devised plan of exclusion – designating and "stamping" Blacks as subhuman to justify slavery and, therein, justifying the deeply entrenched discriminatory laws, policies, and practices that kept Blacks from access to good health, wealth, and freedom. Speaking to the National Book Award Foundation in 2016, Kendi said he wrote the book as a testimony of his faith for an anti-racist America – an America where "Black lives matter." One of Kendi's hopes for the book was to provide a historical view of America that dispels the myth that something is wrong with Black people. I have read Kendi's work and I view it as a heroic effort to interrupt the present-day treatment of Black people and the widespread social exclusion they experience. With this master narrative of exclusion in mind – one of design and purposeful implementation – I write my own reality into existence in this chapter, specifically to unmask and challenge those narratives that have shaped and shaded the humanity of Black children in schools.

The Bronx as a Battlefield

I grew up in the South Bronx. My borough of The Bronx was often talked about differently and despairingly, especially when compared to the other

P.A. Boda (ed.), *Essays on Exclusion*, 39–51.

four boroughs of New York City – Manhattan, Brooklyn, Staten Island, and Queens. Designated as the poorest congressional district in the nation, recent (and historical) data on the South Bronx reports the highest child and adult asthma rates in the nation (Warman, Silver, & Wood, 2009). Labeled by politicians as "the forgotten borough," the Bronx was also often cited as having some of the "worst" schools in New York City. I distinctly remember growing up during the 1980s and hearing these kinds of stories about where I lived, played, and learned to love myself. Somehow these negative narratives were incongruent to what I had experienced, which led me to think about where stories about people and places come from, as well as why they were created in the first place.

As I matured, I learned that when Hollywood and mass media presented their versions of a narrative about my neighborhood in movies like Fort Apache, The Bronx and The Bonfire of the Vanities, someone wanted me to understand that I lived in a "war zone" – on a "battlefield" – a place where death and destruction were commonplace and nothing good could flourish. All of these stories and storylines seemed foreign to me. As a child and young adult, my memories of growing up in the South Bronx were just the opposite of what was presented on the silver screen, circulated in newspapers, and rolled out of the mouths of those who did not live in my community. True, many South Bronxites knew intense financial challenges, political disenfranchisement, and government neglect due to racism, but those myopic and deficit-centered narratives misconstrued the lived experiences my neighbors and I can attest to even years later.

During my childhood, the majority of residents in the South Bronx were Black and Latinx. We lived to tell about the decades of neglect because of politicians who were supposed to support us and bring resources to our community but never fulfilled their promises. This neglect resulted in our poverty and sadness, and often sent many of us into depression and participation in an underground economy, which sometimes led to school dropout and incarceration. It was by design that, in this society, families with children who looked like me were "stamped" just by virtue of how we looked and where we lived as dispensable and uneducable by many who taught in and ran our schools. In our schools, as well as our communities, we were excluded from opportunities that others received as a birthright by those who demarcated the center as their own and our lives as the margins (hooks, 2000).

The exclusion of those in my South Bronx community was the result of a plan perfected over time – a plan intended to keep us and other Black people on the outside, excluded from pursuing "the American Dream," much less actualizing it. I talk about the South Bronx in the ways I experienced it as often as possible in an attempt to offer a counter-narrative to the majoritarian story of my home's imposed narratives of poverty, dejection, and devastation. Notwithstanding its challenges, I remember the South Bronx as a place of warmth and love, filled with laughter and friends (Sealey-Ruiz, 2006). Indeed, there were times when my family and other families struggled, but we found a way because of our love for each other and our community. Despite society's exclusion of us – or perhaps because of it – we pulled together, worked together, and met each other's needs. We did what humans do when faced with seemingly insurmountable collective adversity: We figured out a way. Even though we were meant to be counted out of the game, we still sought to win. In this way, to think about exclusion and its ramifications within education, societal expectations and perceptions of others are required factors to make sense of how exclusion is designed by some and imposed on others for specific purposes.

The Educational Impact of Social Exclusion

As I grew up in the South Bronx, this type of social exclusion presented me with challenges, mostly in school once I left my community. Those of us who attended our neighborhood schools did not receive the finest education. This manifested for me particularly in math and science when I went to high school and college. Social exclusion affects all areas of a person's life. With limitations placed on social resources, those on the "outside" experience life much differently than those who are afforded access to a multitude of resources. Hilary Silver (1995) noted that social exclusion as a construct means that people may be excluded from various forms of economic opportunities that directly impact their livelihood. This lack of cultural capital is further exacerbated by inferior education and overall inhumane treatment that is supported by government policies. Social psychologists are clear about the impact of social exclusion. They have determined that social exclusion affects people's ability to function well, think clearly, and develop deep and close relationships over time. It affects their decision-making, produces sadness, and emerges as a myriad of less-desirable emotions (Twenge, Catanese, & Baumeister, 2002; 2003).

What is also clear and well-documented by researchers is how exclusion occurring within the school environment affects Black children who are members of communities that also experience social exclusion. These children, more than any other group of students, have schooling experiences characterized by access gaps, disproportionate representation in special education programs, and increased participation in a school-to-prison pipeline. Access and opportunity gaps have economic implications, as well, that span beyond just lacking content knowledge. Through a lack of access to rigorous and relevant math and science education, there is a career trajectory gap that creates a scarcity of Blacks working in math, science, engineering, and medical professions, specifically those professions that are linked to economic growth for both individuals and nations (National Center for Education Statistics [NCES], 2013).

Black students who attend schools where achievement gaps and lack of access are prevalent tend to have other interrelated factors contributing to lost opportunities to succeed: teacher inexperience, budgetary constraints, poor resource allocation, unfunded federal mandates, less rigorous curricula, and culturally unresponsive environments. In response to this reality, Milner (2012) suggested five tenets that should be considered when working toward closing access and opportunity gaps in K–12 schools:

- The eradication of color blindness;
- Minimizing cultural conflicts;
- Busting the myth of meritocracy;
- Erasing deficit mindsets that lead to low expectations; and
- Eliminating context-neutral mindsets and practices.

Seemingly by design, schools like the ones in my South Bronx neighborhood perpetuated opportunity and access gaps for the children they served in spite of the wealth of research about how to reach and teach Black students through genuine care and a healthy curiosity about their lives and ways of knowing. Resources in this context were few and of poor quality; above all else, standardized testing was emphasized as the pinnacle goal of learning – the sole measure of educational attainment – even though for decades, educational scholars have purported the need to view students as humans and "whole" children as the crux of democratic teaching and learning.

While my current position in life presents a portrait of "success" – I am a tenured professor at an Ivy League institution – I cannot fully celebrate because for so many children that grew up in my neighborhood, and who attended the same elementary and middle schools I went to more than 35 years ago, have not achieved a high level of success. Many were placed in special education programs and funneled into a school-to-prison pipeline – their chances for success struck down before being fully realized as a process in the making rather than a destination. With this intersectional lean, I depart from the singular narratives that have barred access and stricken hope from some only to empower others. In this way, I take very seriously the charge of encouraging new teachers who may end up teaching in the schools that I attended to adopt the principles Milner (2012) puts forth.

I also ask them to develop their racial literacy, wherein their experiences are examined for their own truths and any misreadings and misunderstandings of others' lived experiences. It is here where the nature of exclusion starts – where some positive, but more often negative, outcomes may come through while interacting with Black children in ways that deny them their humanity. It is also here where I encourage them to examine what happens when their biases materialize for Black students, and what they must do to interrupt their thinking and their behavior.

Exclusion Through Disproportionality: Black Students and Special Education

Over six decades since the "milestone" of integration in the form of the *Brown v. Board of Education* Supreme Court case, there has been and continues to be an overrepresentation of White students in gifted-and-talented programs and a simultaneous disproportionate number of Black children, and most recently Black females (Crenshaw, Ocen & Nanda, 2015; Morris, 2016), in special education programs in relation to their overall enrollment in schools. For over 20 years, researchers have noted that higher rates and significant levels of disproportionality among Black students are found in school districts with predominantly White, middle-class teachers (Gay, 2018). Race and class, as well as the lack of cultural relevance in schools, continue to be mitigating factors that produce exclusion for Black students, leading them to be inappropriately referred to, and classified for, special education in a climate of underrepresented intervention services, resources, access to programs, rigorous curricula, and culturally relevant instruction.

Black students are concurrently underrepresented in gifted, AP (advanced placement), and college-prep classes, and overrepresented on suspension rolls and special education classes for mental retardation, emotional disturbance, and speech impairments. Conversely, White students, particularly when in the same schools as Black students, are overrepresented in gifted, AP, and college-prep classes, and underrepresented in special education classes reserved for "high-risk" categories (Blanchett, 2010). Given these exclusionary practices related to race within special education specifically – that is, most White students are in full-inclusion classrooms, most Black students are in self-contained classrooms – understanding the nature of exclusion through an either/or (i.e., race or disability) analysis fails to encompass the multiplicities occurring at these intersections and the school–prison nexus for those that are multiply marginalized (Annamma, 2017).

In the case of White students, placement in special education is usually initiated by the will of the parent. In this way, racial privilege masks the racism that often causes the disproportionate representation of Black and Brown youth in special education classrooms that is, more often than not, initiated by the student's teacher. There are also distinct differences in outcomes for students who have been placed in special education according to/based on their race. Research has continued to connect the dots to the dangerous outcomes of special education placement by race. Black students in special education are 4.13 times more likely than White students to end up in correctional facilities. Similarly, Annamma, Morrison, and Jackson (2014) found that young Black women growing up in this reality face additional marginalization that can lead to misguided attention on "achievement gaps" rather than on the institutional systems that have led to making these populations vulnerable to this positioning and placement. Indeed, these exclusions are systemic. Therefore, embarking on a path toward equity requires us to use this understanding to address institutional systems that exclude, and in particular address the ways in which Black and Brown students end up in the prison industrial complex because of the biases their teachers' may hold.

Exclusion Through the School-to-Prison Pipeline

The school-to-prison pipeline that exists in U.S. schools because of bloated suspension rolls and the overrepresentation of Blacks (and other students of color) in special education is embedded in a society that leads in rates of incarceration. While the United States is less than 5% of the world's population, it holds almost 25% of the world's total prison population; moreover, it leads all nations in incarceration rates at 716 per 100,000 (Wagner & Sawyer, 2018), and reports these statistics at a time when high school completion rates, particularly for Black males, are at an all-time low of 52% (Schott Foundation, 2015). One must stop and ask the following questions: (1) Why is our country obsessed with incarceration and increasingly laissez-faire when it comes time to address educational disparities? And (2) To what extent do we recognize and understand who is impacted the most by these policies? In this way, understanding the bloated prison population and incarceration rates comes part and parcel with a more thorough understanding of schools as microcosms of larger societal expectations and perceptions, which then play out within disciplinary policies enacted in K–12 education by teachers that may hold racial biases toward Black and Brown youth with or without disabilities.

Research conducted by Skiba and Rausch (2006) has shown that the best indicator for determining who gets suspended from school is not the severity of an infraction, but rather a student's race, previous suspension record, type of school attended, and attendance in special education classes. In addition to being removed from instructional time, a suspended student is, unsurprisingly, more likely to fall behind in classwork, be held over a grade, drop out of high school, commit a crime, and become incarcerated as an adult because of these disproportionately severe disciplinary actions (The Advancement Project, 2005). Moreover, the school-to-prison-pipeline is further fueled by educational inequities through the presence of metal detectors in schools with high populations of Black students (and other students of color), culturally unresponsive curricula, an emphasis on standardized testing, and unfair policing strategies such as racial profiling on school grounds in low-income Black communities – like my former South Bronx neighborhood.

The documentary *13th* directed by Ava Duvernay (*13th*, 2016) and the book *The New Jim Crow: Mass Incarceration in the Age of Colorblindness* (Alexander, 2012) are but two recent examples of our time that add to a long list of scholarship which documents how racist exclusionary and discriminatory practices have led to a disproportionate number of Black men in prison compared with other racial and ethnic groups. There is a glaring connection between schools' zero-tolerance policies that send students to detention and out-of-school suspension for minor infractions (i.e., wearing a hat or other clothing deemed unacceptable in schools) and the school-to-prison pipeline – a "nationwide system of local, state, and federal education and public safety policies that pushes students out of school and into the criminal justice system" (New York Civil Liberties Union, 2007, p. 1). In recent times, the school-to-prison pipeline has had a particularly pernicious impact on the lives of Black girls in schools, which then complicates any analysis of this phenomenon as also intersecting with gender in ways that could not be investigated and prevented unless further considering the intersection of race, class, gender, and disability as they produce exclusion and biasing policies.

From School to Prison and the Pushout of Black Girls

I am a Black female. In New York City, where I was born and raised, Black girls represent 56% of all girls disciplined in schools (Morris, 2016). It should concern us all that 12% of Black girls in pre-kindergarten through 12th grade received an out-of-school suspension during the 2011–12 school year (Crenshaw, Ocen, & Nanda, 2015). In that same year in New York City, for example, 90% of all the girls subjected to expulsion were Black. As fellow citizens of these Black girls, and as educators, we should be disturbed that their suspension rate is six times higher than their White female counterparts. Educators in all schools nationwide should also be concerned that Black girls are three times more likely to attend schools that do not offer the full range of college preparatory courses, and these under-resourced schools are where most teachers fail to meet all state requirements for certification or licensure (Campbell & DeWeever, 2014).

Black girls today, like the Black girl I was during my elementary and middle school years, are exposed to the harsh realities of racism, classism, and sexism. They are even more vulnerable to these multiple marginalizations that design exclusionary practices and policies when disability labeling is considered within this type of intersectional analysis (Annamma, 2017). These factors keep them on the outside of educational opportunities that are given to others as a birthright. These "others" are, of course, demographics that benefit from birthright privileges such as Whiteness, affluence, ableism, and patriarchy – all of which carry substantial capital in the United States and the world writ large, stemming from the colonial project of modernity that utilized difference as a marker of pragmatic and psychological deficit (Fanon, 1952).

This type of exclusion can stop if educators have the courage and will to stop it, and if we as education researchers and teacher educators move our teacher-candidates to develop more intersectional perspectives toward such practices and policies (Sealey-Ruiz, 2011). Researchers, many of whom may be reading this book, are clear that race is the primary reason for these disparities. As with Black boys, Black girls are being educated during an age of mass incarceration, zero-tolerance policies, and harsh treatment by security officers and other school personnel. All of these conditions directly affect their chances for academic success and social inclusion in school. If Black girls are being excluded from school through suspensions and other means, we must be honest as educators that we, and the entire educational system in this country, are deliberately failing them given the massive amount of research that shows us the pragmatic ways that this population is excluded (Annamma, 2017). More importantly, we must hold ourselves accountable if we are complicit in this systematic exclusion and do nothing about it. It is not that educators are not aware of the root causes and how they manifest in schools; however, it is time that we find the moral courage to end the effects of exclusion. If we do not, we will continue to live in a world that one's educational trajectory and life's destiny is heavily influenced by the bodies they are born into rather than the brilliance they develop along their life journey as a function of, and at times in spite of, the experiences that are designed to include and exclude them.

It Shouldn't Take Magic:
Celebrating Black and Female as Humanity

In their 2018 volume of poetry, *Black Girl Magic*, editors Browne, Simmonds and Wood curate a group of Black female poets who, through their art, resist and reject society's litany of restrictions for Black girls. Black girls, and in particular, Black girls that defy White patriarchal ableism, are given the message on a daily basis that they are not supposed to: exist, dream, live freely, or be themselves – their future and narrative of existence is shaped and shaded by those positioning them as not valuable. The title of their book reflects a stance Black girls and women have most recently taken, particularly in the realm of social media, to push back on the social exclusion and outright disrespect and rejection of their existence. It is common for all girls to struggle with confidence; however, Black girls – their pain, their bodies, their very existence – have repeatedly been put on display for observation and critique. The paradox here is that as Black girls are excluded from opportunities in school, and to some extent rendered invisible, there is still a hypervisibility of the Black female as she goes about her daily life (Wallace, 2015).

This burden of always being invisible and simultaneously hypervisible adds to the work with which all Black girls engage as they discover who they are, who they want to be, and how they will travel toward their personal life's journey. Black girls have to constantly work at resisting stories about themselves because so many negative narratives exist, which bombard them and can lead to lacking self-determination. Black girls have to sift through a "mess" of misunderstanding about who they are as they navigate their lives. The idea of Black Girl Magic, (#BlackGirlMagic, Wikipedia, 2018) conceived and made popular by CaShawn Thompson in 2013, intends to celebrate Black girls and women for all they are in the face of adversity, negative storylines, and the threat of social exclusion. As much as I love the term, have used it on several occasions, and will undoubtedly use it again; the beauty, brilliance, triumphs, and challenges of Black girls and women should not be seen as "magic," but as how they simply live out their humanity. Black girls deserve to be acknowledged, included, and seen for all of their complexity of being human. Not magical. Just human. Here we must start our journey toward equity as an intersectional project of action that values young Black female students for their humanity and empowers others to do the same through purposeful design. Only then does the goal of equity become one of designing contexts and institutional systems that ameliorate designed exclusions and let the brilliance of Black youth shine for all to see. To achieve this, we must build new systems of learning centered on this notion of equity.

Combatting Exclusion Through Inclusionary Methods

A move toward inclusion using the culture and experiences of Black students is a step in the right direction. School districts across the nation must implement instruction that matches the knowledge of Black students, and Black girls in particular, with the learning environment. Educators must be encouraged and taught how to embrace a new paradigm and ideology of culture and race/ethnicity as it pertains to their Black students. They must embrace a strengths-based perspective and deliberately reject the stereotypical narratives that lock Black students out of opportunities. The failure of Black students cannot be an option and teachers are the path toward this goal. Schools must create learning environments that reflect the racial and cultural diversity of Black students and affirm that their lives matter. Schools must be deliberate in asking if their Black students feel comfortable and safe, cared for and acknowledged. Given the history of this racist country toward Black people, extra efforts must be put forth to include, not exclude, Black and Brown youth from educational opportunities. Once schools decide to create an ethos that Black Lives Matter, they must continuously analyze student data and send their teachers to professional development that allows them to learn about various learning styles and the actual academic purposes of special education wherein the student is supplied with resources and scaffolds to learn rather than using disability as a proxy argument for the justifiable exclusion of these youth.

Over the years, researchers and practitioners have disputed the view that disproportionate representation is a problem. They have argued that special education placement results in the provision of additional resources and support and should be considered a benefit. However, researchers such as Heller, Holtzman, and Messick (1982) have contended that bias has often been found during the referral process leading to special education placement. Frustratingly and against common belief, Black students in special education are often denied access to general education curriculum and, especially if they have been placed inappropriately in self-contained classrooms with only other students labeled with disabilities, they may receive services that do not meet their needs and be taught by teachers that are not trained in the content they are teaching. This erroneous placement stigmatizes students as inferior, produces lower teacher expectations, and often separates students from peers based on placement – all of which could be ameliorated by general education teachers first and foremost supporting students in ways that draw on these students' assets and cultural capital.

We have adequate research now to show that erroneous and persistent placement in special education leads to poor educational and life outcomes (Patton, 1998). Similar research also shows what inclusion in schools looks like when implemented with the students' learning needs in mind and what social exclusion produces when it is implemented as an inevitable part of a teacher's practice – as something that every teacher will inevitably do (i.e., excluding students and/or recommending them for self-contained instruction). Educators and administrators of schools and school systems need to engage in self-work that leads them to decide if they will be a part of a change that values all children. They must create policies and practices that articulate the belief that all children deserve to be seen and included in ways that matter most. In this way, our goal of equity does not cover up or deny the biases we hold, or the systemic privileges afforded to some and denied to others. Rather, if those individuals who maintain the status quo of systems that oppress and exclude could find their moral compass and initiate change, the goal then becomes an enactment of the very premise of American democracy - an idea that embraces humanity for all.

REFERENCES

13th. (2016). [video] Directed by A. Duvernay. Los Gatos, CA: Netflix.

Alexander, M. (2012). The new Jim Crow: Mass incarceration in the age of colorblindess. New York, NY: The New Press.

Annamma, S. A. (2017). The pedagogy of pathologization: Dis/abled girls of color in the school-prison nexus. New York, NY: Routledge.

Annamma, S., Morrison, D., & Jackson, D. (2014). Disproportionality fills in the gaps: Connections between achievement, discipline and special education in the school-to-prison pipeline. *Berkeley Review of Education*, 5(1), 53-87.

Blanchett, W. J. (2010). Telling it like it is: The role of race, class, and culture in the perpetuation of learning disability as a privileged category for the White middle class. *Disability Studies Quarterly*, 30(2), p.6.

Browne, M.L., Simmonds, I. & Woods, J. (2018). *Black girl magic*. New York, NY: Haymarket Books.

Campbell, M., & Jones DeWeever, A. (2014). *National coalition on Black civic participation Black woman's roundtable report*. Washington, DC: BWR Intergenerational Public Policy Network.

Crenshaw, K., Ocen, P., & Nanda, J. (2015). *Black girls matter: Pushed out, overpoliced, and underprotected*. New York, NY: African American Policy Forum & Center for Intersectionality and Social Policy Studies.

Fanon, F. (1952). *Black skin, White masks*. New York, NY: Grove Press.

Gay, G. (2018). *Culturally responsive teaching: Theory, research, and practice, 3rd Edition.* New York: NY: Teachers College Press.

hooks, b. (2000). *Feminist theory: From margin to center*. New York, NY: Pluto Press.

Kendi, I.X. (2016) *Stamped from the beginning: The definitive history of racist ideas in America*. New York, NY: Nation Books.

Kendi, I.X. (2016). National Book Award [acceptance speech]. Retrieved from http://www.nationalbook.org/nba2016winner_nf_kendi-stamped-from-the-beginning.html#.WzjXA1MvzL8

Milner, IV, R. H. (2012). Beyond a test score: Explaining opportunity gaps in educational practice. *Journal of Black Studies*, 43, 693-718.

Morris, M. (2016). *Pushout: The criminalization of Black girls in schools*. New York, NY: The New Press.

Heller, K. A., Holtzman, W. H., Messick, S., & National Research Council (U.S.). (1982). *Placing children in special education: A strategy for equity*. Washington, D.C: National Academy Press.

New York Civil Liberties Union. (2007). "School to prison pipeline fact sheet". Retrieved from: http://www.nyclu.org/publications/fact-sheet-school-prisonpipeline-2007.

Wagner, P. & Sawyer, W. & Prison Policy Initiative (2018). *States of incarceration: The global context*. https://www.prisonpolicy.org/global/. Massachusetts.

Patton, J. M. (1998). The disproportionate representation of African Americans in special education: Looking behind the curtain for understanding and solutions. *The Journal of Special Education*, 32, 1, 25 – 31.

Schott Foundation. (2015). Black lives matter: The Schott 50-state report on public education and Black males. Retrieved from http://www.blackboysreport.org.

Sealey-Ruiz, Y. (2006). Getting to here from there: One woman's journey from the South Bronx to the academy. *WILLA Journal, National Council of Teachers of English*, 14, 40-42.

Sealey-Ruiz, Y. (2011). Dismantling the school-to-prison pipeline through racial literacy development in teacher education. *Journal of Curriculum and Pedagogy*, 8, 116-120.

Silver, H. (1995). Reconceptualizing social disadvantage: three paradigms of social exclusion. In G. Rodgers, C. Gore, & J. B. Figueiredo (Eds.), *Social exclusion: Rhetoric, reality, responses* (pp. 58-80). Institute of International Labour Studies: Geneva.

Skiba, R. J., & Rausch, M. K. (2006). Zero tolerance, suspension, and expulsion: Questions of equity and effectiveness. In C. M. Evertson & C. S. Weinstein (Eds.), *Handbook of classroom management: Research, practice, and contemporary issues* (pp. 1063-1089). Mahwah, NJ, US: Lawrence Erlbaum Associates Publishers.

Twenge, J. M., Catanese, K. R., & Baumeister, R. F. (2002). Social exclusion causes self-defeating behavior. *Journal of Personality and Social Psychology*, 83, 606-615.

Twenge, J. M., Catanese, K. R., & Baumeister, R. F. (2003). Social exclusion and the deconstructed state: Time perception, meaninglessness, lethargy, lack of emotion, and self-awareness. *Journal of Personality and Social Psychology*, 85, 409-423.

Wallace, M. (2015) *Black Macho and the Myth of the Superwoman*, Reprint. New York, NY: Verso.

Warman, K., Silver, E. J., & Wood, P. R. (2009). Modifiable risk factors for asthma morbidity in Bronx versus other inner-city children. *Journal of Asthma*, 46, 995-1000.

Wikipedia (2018, June 21, updated). "Black girl magic". https://en.wikipedia.org/wiki/Black_Girl_Magic

Chapter 3

EXCLUSION BY DESIGN

The Rhetoric and Material Realities that Construct Difference

Phillip A. Boda

Whether we recognize it or not, everything around us has come into existence through a design created by someone else – a thought that was then drawn up and subsequently pushed into the world with particular intents in mind. I do not mean the proverbial 'act of God'-creationist argument, rather that once 'stuff' existed on Earth, we humans manipulated it for our own betterment, or at the very least the betterment of a particular group of people we assessed as the primary focus for deserving to be a recipient of such designs. It is a quandary to think about: If we manipulate and design our world for the better, why are we in such a chaotic epoch right now? Why is it such that people around the world experience these designs differently, and what does that mean for us living in America? Leaving the more ethereal and global argument for others much more qualified, I, instead, focus on the nature of exclusion as it has manifested in American schools through the arguments and actions that are designed to define difference as deficit – i.e., the rhetoric and material realities of exclusion that can teach us how to collectively create educational equity *by design* rather than happenstance or grandiose speculations of abstract philosophy without pragmatic action.

To this end, what we are really talking about are three interwoven pieces to this puzzle related to narrative, design, and experience: namely,

1. Present-day educational expectations have emerged from people who have many different personal experiences;

P.A. Boda (ed.), *Essays on Exclusion*, 53–63.

2. These educational designs can be attributed to particular arguments about who is intended to benefit from their proposed outcomes; and

3. Through our experiences, we have been exposed to specific stories about how schooling should work, does work, and why, which inevitably justify actions we take to sustain particular ways of our students embodying an American citizen.

It is with these tenets in mind that we start our journey to understand how exclusion in American schools is justified as the standard answer to the diverse bodies of students, and their teachers charged to serve them, interacting together, as well as how we can collectively redesign educational rhetoric and the material realities that these students and teachers face on a daily basis to embody more equitable policy and practices to counteract this exclusion. Indeed, as experiences are as varied as there are people living in the world, the primary purpose of critical work toward equity in education is to expose and educate those that may not have purview to the nature of exclusion – pulling back the veil of subversive discrimination that haunts those defined as 'different' to re-story narratives for those that wish to hear experiences beyond their own, to truly listen. But first, let's take a step back and reflect on our own experiences in relation to schooling, and to model that process I provide my own narrative of interaction with exclusion from a couple of experiences – to shed light on the power of narrative re-storying and how I make sense of it in my own personal interpretations of schooling spaces, and the world writ large.

What Happens Within Schools? A Personal Account of Learning Difference

Schools are microcosms of societies more broadly and since we all have had experiences in schools, we all have different stories to tell about the purpose of schooling, or lack thereof. In my experiences – the only positionality (Mensah, 2016) I can authentically speak from – schooling was a way to make sense of other people. Coming from a pretty insular family with little connection to other (or diverse) families in terms of recreation and social gatherings, I learned about people different from myself through my time in schools, as a student and a teacher. I find it odd when I look back and think about the narratives I learned concerning people that were unlike my own family – the stories I was told and the experiences I had interacting with people different from me. These experiences not only exposed me to the stories my family adopted to make sense of the world, but also the stories other families told their children to make sense of their place within society when juxtaposed to anyone unlike themselves.

These stories explain for youth their expected relationship with children that are visibly and/or invisibly different and/or neurodivergent (Ashby & Woodfield, 2019) from them, or those marked positionalities identified within a social group that are expected to be seen as abhorrent based on the expectation of normality. In other words, as children learn difference, they are doing so as an active interaction with the rhetoric (stories) that their families have told them about what it means to be different, as well as the material realities (actions) that position those identified as different as being (more often than not) 'less-than' the image of one's Self and familial culture. Two of my own experiences provide exemplary stories and actions of this type of indoctrination into 'normal' to elaborate on the idea that rhetoric leads to material realities of exclusion – both in the minds of youth and the prejudicial alliances they create that enforce discriminatory praxes.

Learning Racism

I vividly remember being in elementary school on the playground for recess, about first or second grade, and having two white boys that I knew tell me to go up to a Black girl in our grade and yell a racial slur while beating a stick on the ground chasing her – you know the racial slur, I need not explicitly state it here. I didn't do it because I did not understand the slur at the time but knew enough to recognize when I may be replicating something hurtful onto someone else given the way the boys proposed their suggestion – a jest of sorts. When I got home, I wanted to 'test' that story and performed it in front of my dad and brother while we were walking up the driveway, and their reactions were pure astonishment. They told me not to say that word, scolded me for it, and my brother just shook his head – as if I was supposed to know what that word meant even if I had never heard it before. Indeed, this is a place where my privilege shines bright: not to have to learn that word because it didn't affect me, and I acknowledge that here, first and foremost.

Later on in my life, and through more 'educational' experiences in and out of schools, I learned what that word meant, as well as why I should not say it, but in the moment that I enacted it I didn't learn anything – there was a silent expectation that it was negative and, thus, shouldn't be said, at least not in public spaces or for anyone to hear. As a reader, pause for a moment and think about your past 'educational' experiences:

- Have you ever experienced such an implicit story being told about other people?
- What experiences have framed your views of others when thinking about your youth?

These stories are present in all familial interactions – silent and salient, sometimes, but always embodied, enforced, and taught through performance – and we all need to think about them as we move forward in our journey to interrogate difference and exclusion. What this experience, and subsequent reflection, taught me was that there were stories told to these white boys about Black folks (and probably Brown folks, as well), and that they would inevitably tell/enact those stories to/with others explicitly and implicitly. Indeed, these stories did not originate out of happenstance; these unquestioned logics of Othering and representation define the colonial approach to cultural genocide and assimilatory praxes that deny subjectivity over the past hundreds of years (Fanon, 1963; Mignolo, 2007), and are arguably still seeded in our institutional discourses and practices today. This experience also taught me another lesson: While I was a mixed-race boy, I could pass for white, and I wasn't Black; therefore, the derogatory comment used against the young Black girl need not apply to me. What a story to be told and learned – in a primary schooling context nonetheless!

Even as these white boys did not explicitly state the meaning of the racial slur, I would soon learn it, perform it as a test of clarity with those closest to me, and find out if it was one of the stories that my family believed was true and appropriate to use when speaking about others not like me. Soon enough, I had to decide if that story was for me, as well as if it was appropriate for my own identity as a mixed-race youth growing up on a side of my family that was resoundingly aligned to whiteness and white culture. I also had to recognize what this story meant in terms of who I was as a person – my identity and cultural alliances – in relation to those different from me. Was this the best way that I should approach people that were different from me – to point out that difference in ways that would make those defined as different feel like less than, as jests of their identity that should be highlighted and mocked as needing of change? Should I defer any outward projection of bias towards others but never really think about what it means to my identity and family?

These stories, like many others told in this volume, are complicated and, yes, they relate to everyone, everywhere, who seek to find out where they 'fit' in the world as it exists. This is the nature of how we begin to understand our place in the world: How our peers and family narrate people different from us and where we find ourselves in that story in relation to them – we find (i.e., define) ourselves in relation to the words of others, and our consciousness is borne out of that interaction (Bahktin, 2010). This is how we build weak and strong social connections as a functionality of place and interaction, particularly in 'superdiverse' contexts (Phillimore, Humphries, Klaas, & Knecht, 2016).

Experiences such as this happen all the time, and I have had my share of experimentation in terms of understanding difference across my lifetime both in and out of schools. What is important to note here, though, is that the essence of this experience is not unique to me, nor is it unique to anyone living in America. However, given that our country often seeks to emphasize the idea that we are 'American above all else,' it is hard to think about the differences that exist between peoples in America – this is the story we adopt, and the one we perform every day. Through this rhetoric of an all-encompassing identity marker of 'American,' we mask the material realities that produce particular racist (in this example) enactments that hark back to Jim Crow era America – an exemplary model to justify the validity of the bootstrap ideology, indeed.

Furthermore, if we are all encompassed under the label 'American,' shouldn't we also be treated the same? Shouldn't these stories about difference never even exist because 'we don't see difference' and 'just see American'? Given that this is NOT the case in America (given whatever measure you would like to use as a litmus test), suffice it to say that difference – and, therein, bias based on the idea of difference in relation to yourself – is embedded within the stories we tell (our rhetoric about who is, indeed, 'American-enough') and the actions we then enact that produce pragmatic material realities affecting the lives of others. This race-based form of discrimination is not the only experience I had with exclusion, though, and not the last to showcase the deep-seeded bigotry passed down among generations under the guise of what it means to be 'normal.'

Learning Homophobia

I was in high school when I had more experiences that dealt with the nature of schooling being deeply connected to personal stories that families told their children and their influence on my own identity coming from a mixed-race, and (at the time closeted) queer identity. I was in a history class – one of those 30+ student classes required to graduate – and taking it a year ahead of my classmates, which meant I was surrounded by students one year ahead of me. Needless to say, I was a bit timid and tried my best to go unnoticed. I sat in front of someone who I perceived as a 'cool' male student (given his hyper-masculine and chauvinistic bravado that was commended by all – teachers and students alike) and next to a timid male student like myself. I remember two instances that play off of one another, which represent the nature of stories being told explicitly and implicitly about 'normal,' acceptable studenthood in my school. In these instances, what was constructed as 'normal' was not just something theoretical, it was pragmatic and generated from a specific action about who was accepted, and therein valued, within the school.

The first was when this 'macho' student made a joke about the timid student, stating to me that the timid student was 'staring at my crotch' and I should 'watch out.' What one does in a moment such as this defines your identity in relation to particular alliances with the parties involved, for all parties involved. As a not-yet-out queer youth (both to myself and others), I hesitated and decided to ignore it out of fear of recognition of my own subconscious relation to queerness – I laughed it off as if not to call any attention to my own sexual confusion. The timid student was, in fact, self-identified as gay, and that leads to the next instance. The queer, timid student raised his hand one day to get the attention of the teacher, who proceeded to ask what the student wanted from his desk across the room – no need to get up, you know, because teachers should always stay seated to address students ::cough:: horrible teacher move ::cough::.

Anyway, the queer student replied, 'He's making fun of me,' to which the teacher asked 'Why,' and in a low voice, but just loud enough for the teacher to hear from across the room, the student said 'because I'm Gay.' WOAH! What a heroic stand! He "outed" himself publicly – I had never seen or heard of such an act before in my life. The teacher's subsequent response was to shake his head in disgust, making a noise to emphasize this recognition that this student said something vile (and subsequently was someone abhorrent), and disregarded that the complaint was ever made, going about his business while the student body laughed. Right then and there, I knew that coming out was not an option for me, nor was being gay 'okay' in that teacher's eyes, or the eyes of my classmates who so blatantly followed suit in their disregard to a student/teacher's bigotry.

This experience taught me that being gay meant that you were open to, at the very least, verbal harassment, with no subsequent authority to go to in such an occurrence for reassurance that you would be protected from such abuse. In essence, to be out in America, as I learned through this experience, meant that it was an every-second-of-every-day possibility that you would be harassed – physically, emotionally, and spiritually – and that there was nothing you could do about it: There was no one to call for protection, no one to rely on for security during a period of time when youth are trying to make sense of their place in the world, and that even if there was someone that could support you, they couldn't be with you all the time – defining 'protective social capital' as contextually dependent and not always available. This consequence, again, is learned, not inherent in the fabric of what it means to be human, or what it means to be a citizen of a nation-state, such as being 'American.' Indeed, if we define 'American' as a constitutionalist would, we all have the right to life, liberty, and the pursuit of happiness without the threat of outside imposition.

* * *

Through these two experiences, the nature of the differences represented therein (not heterosexual, not white) were placed in juxtaposition to normal as a function of a very specific, and negative, learned rhetoric of difference, and then treated as such through particular realities pushed into the world as the appropriate – and dare I say, designed – responses that students will face if they embody this departure from normal, creating exclusion as a material piece of our social interactions derived explicitly from our personal experiences with Self, community, and context. This derives from an acceptance of stories about ourselves as 'normal' and the defining of Others as 'abnormal,' as well as 'in need' of assimilating into 'normal' through particular biocultural markers (Davis, 2014). I would soon learn later on in my undergraduate degree that physical assault was also not a priority for the American judicial system when my own cases of gay-bashing were not pursued, as well as through the countless lives of LGTBQ+ Americans that lose their lives and their rights under the bigotry of others every day, to this day.

Constructing Normal: A Synthesis

These experiences taught me stories about being 'normal,' and about difference in relation to race and sexuality. First, that if you are macho or want to build alliances with those types of students often seen through favorable eyes by white hetero-patriarchally aligned teachers and students, you make fun of, and actively try to point out flaws in, anyone that is different from the 'normal' student embodiment related to what those students/teachers deem as 'normal' – here, that would be white and heterosexual. The reader might now stop and say, 'Well, that's just boys being boys – it's part of growing up – we all did it!' or, 'It's natural to point out differences and form bonds with people that are like you.' To this, I respond not in judgment, but in revelation: This act of 'focusing on differences' and 'discriminating against them' is, at its foundation, derived from a set of experiences youth have with their family, peers, and mentors in relation to how they model interacting with difference as being deficit.

What I am pointing out is that this way of thinking about how to respond and interact with difference is first and foremost modeled and, therein, taught through the experiences young people have, and the subsequent discussions that happen if and when they decide to discuss such experiences with the modeler of that action – traditionally role models, community mentors, and/or family members. The arguments about these actions – the rhetoric justifying this exclusive mentality toward difference – is a reflection of the consequences that youth are exposed to when difference plays out in front of them in social contexts when they are growing up.

To rephrase in a simpler explanation, when Blackness and homosexuality were first presented to these youth, they looked to their peers, community, and family members to determine how to make sense and respond to these forms of difference that they were never exposed to before that moment. The response they observed became a story told to them about how to both think and act when they encounter that form of difference on their own. This leads to a replication of that rhetoric (that story) into performed material realities (actions of discrimination) where 'Othered' youth (and 'Othered' people in general) are positioned by that youth as different, and therein deficit, from their own identity as 'normal.' To be 'abnormal' is then to be 'in need' of something to make you more 'normal,' more white or heterosexual, as it were, in this set of experiences that have taught me about 'normal.'

Through these experiences, I learned what stories other people told their children about how to be a student, who may or may not be considered a 'normal' student (or even human, in that respect), and reasons why people would be ostracized from a label of being a normal student in American schools. For those that are reading this and believe that these experiences may be anecdotal, or even dated, I would encourage you to talk to queer youth, or the quiet kids in your classrooms, or the students of color that go to predominantly white schools, or immigrant students labeled as English Language Learners, or

Muslim students in a largely 'Christian'-populated public school – this is not, and has not, been an exception to the norm that we sustain and obey.

These are the stories that our children believe are true because of the experiences they have interacting with the rhetoric of difference in America that produces extremely traumatic and violent material realities for students different from the English-speaking, white, Christian, male, heterosexual, affluent norm – with all the cues and expectations that come with this image related to the particular geographical histories where this idea of 'normal' derives itself. In saying this, we must also recognize that these stories came from somewhere; these narratives about people came from experiences and from people these children trusted telling them that this is how to react to difference. These actions and responses were, by cultural design, embodied in the stories we tell our children through nonverbal responses to difference and direct communication of hateful rhetoric; these are the exclusive identities that shape what the normal student is supposed to be, and not supposed to be, in American schools. Moreover, these are exclusions that were designed by society more broadly, and both students and teachers alike perform them in schools.

Given these experiences, and a bit of elaboration on them in relation to stories that exclude, what we see are fundamental examples of exclusion that are widely reported throughout educational research and sociology - a glimpse to how individual experiences and responses shape exclusion in relation to race and sexuality. Thus, my central argument is based on the rhetoric and material reality of 'normal' as a juxtaposition to 'difference' that is pervasively used within education to exclude Black and Brown youth, as well as other students marked as different who depart from the idea of normal, through a systematic coding of difference as embodying a disability incarnate. Through this *exclusion by design* being part of a process to define difference as inherently deficit, race and disability become interwoven within the same cloth of discrimination. Students' 'abnormally labeled' identities – the imposed ones that teachers, administration, and even those parents supplant onto them – then become aligned with the notion of deficit in relation to a white Westernized notion of normal. Black and Brown youth are subsequently seen as placeholders and proxy juxtapositions to the normal white studenthood emphasized in American schools to maintain the normative center of schools through excluding those who do not 'fit' within that norm (Leonardo & Broderick, 2011) – anyone not embodying whiteness and able-bodiedness.

Therefore, whiteness and ableism, historically and presently, have and are still aligned with a colonizer mentality wherein to be 'not white' or 'not able' is also to be seen as 'uncivilized,' 'backward,' and 'inherently deficit.' Whiteness and ability, and by transference, American-ness, is thus defined as the 'normal,' as the center to which all peoples in the margins should strive to become. Whoever departs from this Americanity (Quijano & Wallerstein, 1992) incarnate is therefore seen as lacking the biocultural markers that define normal as a goal to strive for – they embody a lacking ability to achieve white American-ness; these differences then become signified as disabilities, as deficits to eradicate or obfuscate.

To continue this excavation of biocultural rhetoric and realities, and for us to understand what the argument of acceptance means in terms of exclusion in American schools, we must also take a look at the components that often define 'inclusion' in positive ways but are subversively negative. Acceptance through this lens is then divided into the previous two parts that carry with them derogatory denotations: Ability and Achievement. On the one hand, we have acceptance and ability – if students have the ability to assimilate into roles and identities that are deemed 'normal' (i.e., white and able, therein, assumed as biologically superior via eugenic rhetoric), they can be accepted. On the other hand, we have acceptance and achievement – if students can't assimilate into 'normal,' white and able identities, but can succeed within standardized measures of achievement that 'normal' students succeed on, they can be accepted, at least on the basal level of acceptance for their individual achievement, but are still not seen as representative of the demography they may be a part of – non-white and/or disabled. Here is where we should problematize this notion that acceptance and inclusion is enough to define equity as productively being taken up within American schools.

Conclusive Remarks

The premise for this chapter was to engage the reader on a cognitive and affective quest to interrogate how difference is constructed rhetorically and materially as a deficit. In it, readers have been presented with personal narratives and over-arching theories about exclusion, difference, and the concept of normal so that they can start to think about how to engage with the rhetoric of these myths and how they are dependent on actively disregarding and denying the humanity of others. The rhetoric and material realities that have been presented here, and throughout the rest of this volume, provide a glimpse into the fact that exclusion is purposefully designed for particular groups of students – those defined as abnormal, different, and therein less than those who are 'normal.' Indeed, those students that choose not to, or do not have the capability to make a choice to, abide by the normal 'white' and 'able' identities of a student deserving acceptance, particularly those marked by difference and disability as being inherently deficit, are held individually accountable for their perceived shortcoming, devoid of systemic and prejudicial factors (Annamma, Connor, & Ferri, 2013). And this claim is time-and-time again seen within other authors' stories about exclusion in American schools. It is with this premise that this volume seeks to present and interrogate both our own personal work to disrupt this hierarchal model of humanity, as well as provide narratives that speak truth to power (Sium & Ritskes, 2013) in ways that the reader may not know about yet. In turn, we argue for a humanity that is inclusion not because of demanded expectations of normality, but because of the fundamental premise of love and care. Without such a charge, our educational systems will continue to perpetuate the system in which it is designed to sustain, in all its forms of exclusion and superficial inclusion under the guise of normal – thereby willingly accepting the construction of exclusion by design in our schools.

References

Annamma, S. A., Connor, D., & Ferri, B. (2013). Dis/ability critical race studies (DisCrit): Theorizing at the intersections of race and dis/ability. *Race Ethnicity and Education, 16*, 1-31.

Ashby, C., & Woodfield, C. (2019). Honouring, Constructing and Supporting Neurodivergent Communicators in Inclusive Classrooms. In K. Scorgie & C. Forlin (Eds.), *Promoting Social Inclusion: Co-Creating Environments that Foster Equity and Belonging* (pp. 151-167). Emerald Publishing Limited.

Bakhtin, M. M. (2010). *Speech genres and other late essays.* University of Texas Press.

Fanon, F. (1963). *The wretched of the earth.* New York: Grove Press.

Davis, L. (2014). *The end of normal: Identity in a biocultural era.* Ann Arbor: University of Michigan Press.

Fanon, F. (1963). *The wretched of the earth.* New York: Grove Press.

Leonardo, Z., & Broderick, A. (2011). Smartness as property: A critical exploration of intersections between Whiteness and disability studies. *Teachers College Record, 113*, 2206-2232.

Mensah F.M. (2016) Positional identity as a framework to studying science teacher identity. In L. Avraamidou (Ed.), *Studying science teacher identity: New directions in mathematics and science education* (p.49-69). Rotterdam, The Netherlands: Sense Publishing.

Mignolo, W. D. (2007). Introduction: Coloniality of power and de-colonial thinking. *Cultural Studies, 21*, 155-167.

Mignolo, W. (2011). *The darker side of western modernity: Global futures, decolonial options.* Duke University Press.

Oliver, K. (2004). *The colonization of psychic space: A psychoanalytic social theory of oppression.* U of Minnesota Press.

Phillimore, J., Humphries, R., Klaas, F., & Knecht, M. (2016). *Bricolage: potential as a conceptual tool for understanding access to welfare in superdiverse neighbourhoods.* IRiS Working Paper Series 14. Birmingham: Institute for Research into Superdiversity.

Quijano, A., & Wallerstein, I. (1992). 'Americanity as a concept,' or the Americas in the modern world. *International Social Science Journal, 44*, 549-557.

Sium, A., & Ritskes, E. (2013). Speaking truth to power: Indigenous storytelling as an act of living resistance. *Decolonization: Indigeneity, Education & Society, 2*(1), I-X.

Chapter 4

WHY CAN'T YOU SEE US?

The Visibilization of Blackwomen and BlackQueer Folx

SHAMARI REID & CATHRYN DEVEREAUX

Shamari's Narrative

Some Sundays I (Shamari) would be lucky enough that my mother would reward my stale performance of feigning to be exhausted with allowing me to skip out on church to continue sleeping; to continue dreaming of a world in which my BlackQueer life and love mattered. I have every reason to believe that my mother knew I was an insomniac and rarely felt tired. But she let me stay home anyway, some Sundays. Some Sundays, she would wrap her egg and sausage sandwich, Blue and Gold sausage only, in a paper towel and head to church. Baptist church, so, chile, you know she was dressed to the nines, as Easter Sunday came every week in our house. And every week she would be showered with, "Girl, I'm scared of you" and, "Gone wit yo bad self."

Mama knew, I think, what going to church did to me, and how it gave life and hope to her and other churchgoers, but left me feeling everything but saved and sanctified. Mama knew, I think, that church was where I first performed self-erasure, fading into the milieu of three-part harmonies, holy water, grandmothers' pearls, and gaudy hats topped with feathers, enwrapped by ribbon, and trimmed in lace. I assume that my mother also knew that it was in church, because of the congregation's narrow interpretation of the bible, where I perfected the art of tying a tie. Either way, today wouldn't be one of those special Sundays where I could spend

P.A. Boda (ed.), *Essays on Exclusion*, 65–84.

my afternoon creating stories about magical Blackgirls, joyous Black boys, invisible genderless Black children, and dragonflies. This Sunday morning, she would respond to my ritual monologue about fatigue with, "We're leaving this house at 10:45."

I would take my time putting on my "church clothes," which were constricting and incongruent with my soul. Dress shirt. I would tie my tie, just as my late aunt had taught me, simple knot. Of course, a Blackwoman taught me how to tie a tie, she too had learned that self-preservation for us was synonymous with self-erasure, an idea I return to later in the chapter. I would embellish my aunt's instructions with the additional life-preserving tips about tying a knot I picked up from wandering around in a society that vilified things it did not fully understand, things like queer love.

I would place the tie around my neck. Adjust the wider end so that it hung lower than the skinny end, just as my narrowly defined masculinity would have to hang lower than my undervalued femininity today. I was going to church. Cross the wide end over the small end. Keep the Beyoncé references to a minimum and un-remember everything learned from Tyra about *werking* the runway. I was going to church. Place two fingers over the wide end. Lower your voice; be mindful of the ways you move your wrists, and never roll the eyes. Bring the wide end around the two fingers and behind, up into, then down through the loop. Do this with the same flair demonstrated in last night's game by popular basketball players whose names were dangerous to forget. Remember: It is very important that you only manipulate the wider, more masculine end; the skinny feminine side must remain idle. And if you have executed this knot successfully, the skinny end will remain invisible, concealed by the masculine end. An illusion that could save your life. You're going to church. Slacks. Belt. Dress shoes. Cufflinks: optional.

Church began at 11. We arrived at 11:03. The choir's harmonies would fill me up. Music could do that. When they were using their voices to worship to their God, I felt ephemeral love. I could loosen my tie just a bit. Today's sermon would lift up the Black struggle. The pastor began: "Church, I've come here on today to tell you that oppression is real." Amen. And the pastor would continue, reminding us that we were loved even though we were Black because God loved all of his children. To which the congregation would respond, "Amen." He would preach that our lives mattered. Our struggles were real and not self-created. Racism was not imagined. Amen. He would charge us all to love each other and our neighbors. Amen. By this time, folks would be on their feet. Then, he would talk about the strength of the most important character in the Black story, the (cisgender-heterosexual) Black man. AMEN!

His exclamation that "Blackwomen need Black men" would be met with a chorus of "hallelujahs" and "preach, pastor." That's how we make this right. Y'all don't hear me. A woman and a man. That's how it was all intended. And let the church say collectively: Amen. Homosexuality is just wrong and has no place in our communities. It ain't nothing but the devil. I would look around to see if there was anyone, who like me would only mouth "amen" but feel so asphyxiated that there would be no air to help such toxic language escape their throat. I had been forsaken. Everyone else let "amen" ring all up and through that church. Their God surely heard them. My tie was too tight. In that moment, the act of telling your neighbor you loved them at the top of the service felt hollow. They didn't love me. They didn't even see me. It was very clear that my struggle was not the Black struggle. If they were excluded from political participation in society and disenfranchised for their raced beings, as someone who lived in that same skin and loved queerly, what was I? At age 8, I was unable to answer that question, but at least I knew how to tie a tie.

On Blackwomen

It is axiomatic that if we do not define ourselves for ourselves, we will be defined by others – for their use and to our detriment. (Lorde, 2007/1984, p. 45)

For centuries, Blackwomen have confronted the pressures of upholding Eurocentric standards of beauty and feminism, like long, straight hair and fair skin – trauma which dates back to American slavery when enslaved Black folx were separated by skin tone and allotted labor assignments accordingly: darker skin indicating manual labor (field negroes), while lighter skin indicating domestic work (house negroes) (Davis, 2017). These messages, passed down through generations, condemning coarse hair and dark skin, are further perpetuated by mainstream media, teaching Blackwomen and girls to leave our natural selves at home and be something else more appropriate.

At an early age, Blackgirls internalize these messages, finding few places of refuge where they are free to be their authentic selves. Even in schools, institutions that should praise their uniqueness and honor the diversity they embody, Blackgirls are often policed and punished when they do not cater to teachers' and school leaders' racialized, classed, and gendered constructions of femininity (Hines-Datiri & Carter Andrews, 2017). When Blackgirls are independent, assertive, expressive, and bold in school, they are often read as deviant, disrespectful, and disruptive. This misreading of Blackgirls in schools becomes even further complicated when implicit and explicit biases, excessive surveillance, zero-tolerance policies, and exclusionary discipline practices are in place. Here, Blackgirls are not only excluded and pushed out, they are marginalized, criminalized, and invisibilized (Morris, 2016).

From banning braids and natural hairstyles to vague and subjective language in school policies and codes of conduct (like "inappropriate" and "disrespectful"), schools have become unsafe places for Blackgirls who are often subjected to stakeholders that lack cultural competence and gender responsiveness. Thus, amidst coming of age, Blackgirls must decide whether they will opt to be true to themselves, even if it means rejection, or conforming to the Eurocentric standards society forces upon them.

With mass movements underway encouraging us to #ReclaimOurTime, our bodies, our minds, our culture, and our hair, Blackwomen and girls are working tirelessly to change the narrative and heal. Movies like *Hidden Figures* (2016) and *Nappily Ever After* (2018) that celebrate and uplift Blackwomen's stories, lives, beauty, and strength, while few and far in-between, encourage us to keep up the fight of both self-defense and self-love, embrace our #BlackGirlMagic, and remember that #BlackGirlsRock. The trauma is real; it runs deep, and it must be undone. We must uphold our responsibility of self-definition or else risk losing ourselves in what others demand for us. The following narrative depicts my experience as a teenage Blackgirl discovering of my lost, erased self as I tried to conform to what society told me I should be.

Kat's Narrative

I (Kat) arose, wild-haired and dizzy, as sun rays crept through the bends of my dusty blinds proclaiming the day anew, nightfall a thing of the past, and tomorrow one step closer. I stretched my arms up to the Heavens releasing the stillness of my slumber. It was time to prepare my body and mind yet again. I could feel the anxiety creeping up from the depths of my belly, but letting it devour me was not an option. I didn't like school very much and that was no secret, so every day took convincing and I wore the task relentlessly like a promise ring to remind myself of my unwavering commitment to education and perseverance because my mama and my mama's mama showed me so.

I went through my morning routine of teeth brushing, face washing, and showering off yesterday like business as usual. I saturated my melanated skin with cocoa butter because it always held me down and kept me from the whiteness of ash. I put on the white skirt and black shirt my best friend told me to wear so we could match, as if our all-White private school needed another reason to label us indistinguishable. As if we needed more than our Blackgirlhood to unite us. As if it was easier to make it through the day twinning than to let the world know we actually had our own distinct identities.

I combed through my half-permed hair, dividing curly coils at the roots and straight strands towards the ends – doubly conscious and navigating conflicting terrain, just like me, just like my Blackwomanness required, just as Du Bois proclaimed. Apart from hating hair salons because the dryers were always too hot and the overall process took forever and a day, I never really liked how straight hair looked on me. I came to love the apple biting sounds my kinky roots made as they popped through the teeth of a comb, but not enough to let go of the perm on the ends that reminded me of what that world deemed appropriate for a Blackgirl like me. I slabbed on thick layers of JAM to keep my edges intact, and then brushed down my curls until they were flat enough to mask their true nature and behaved well enough to fit neatly inside of my elastic scrunchie. I knew to tie my hair down with a scarf for at least 10 minutes before leaving, just to make sure my edges knew I meant business. It was what I had been trained to do. It's what kept White folks from asking too many questions. It's what kept them comfortable, and me inconspicuous. They wanted to touch my braids when I wore them, and while I loved braids, I hated being treated like an exhibit; hated having to explain; hated having to be polite.

I fastened my favorite silver hoop earrings into each ear and strutted over to the mirror to view the finished product. My eyes met the glass, and I awaited the moment when I'd look back at myself from the other side, except, there was no other side. I could see straight through it as if the mirror had become a window. No one was there to look back at me. I searched for myself, my face, my eyes, or anything that would let me know I was actually there. That I was real. That I existed. As moments passed, I watched hope float further and further away like balloons slipping from my hands on a windy day and being claimed by the sky. The searching pained my eyes like the sun through dusty blinds. I had no choice but to walk away. Invisible in my own skin, I wondered if I'd ever come back. I wondered if I was ever really here in the first place. I wondered, if I couldn't even see me, then who could?

I walked out of my bedroom door, coming to grips with idea of being unnoticed and unseen by the world around me. Losing myself was the hardest part. I had already been in circles that chose not to see me: White folks who never really tried to get to know me, either assuming that they already did or not concerning themselves with the idea that they didn't; White girls who exoticized me; White women who pitied my Blackness and assumed I yearned for their Whiteness; Black boys who saw my body, but only saw my body; Black men who valued the voices of other men the most... Yes, I had been unnoticed and unseen. I didn't like how it felt, but I learned not to expect more from them. Would I have to learn not to expect more from me as well? How had I gotten to this place? How long had I been gone? Was this the first time I realized I was missing? I didn't know then that there were a host of other missing Blackgirls. I hadn't noticed. I suppose many people hadn't noticed either. How long had we been invisible?

As I made my way to the front door to await the yellow bus that would carry me back into the White world that school allowed me access into, my mother called out, "Kat, don't forget your breakfast! You need to eat something." I pivoted into the kitchen to grab a sausage, egg and cheese Hot Pocket out the freezer and pop it into the microwave, quick and easy. In two minutes time, the Hot Pocket was ready, and as I went to grab it, I came to a powerful realization: The world may not see me. I may not see myself. But my mama always saw me.

Merging Our Narratives

In analyzing our experiences, as a BlackQueer man and a Blackwoman, we have arrived at the sobering realization that our memories of schooling are not constituted solely by recollections of exclusion, but also present moments of erasure. It is our intention with this chapter to a) share our lives as to approximate a more nuanced understanding of our experiences of exclusion (read: erasure) as members of groups who are often left to lead lives in the margins of the margins, and b) complicate the myopic narratives being told about Black youth, LGBTQ+ youth, and girls. It also warrants stating that we do not maintain that our stories will speak to the lives of all who may identify as we do, rather we offer our narrative accounts as a departure point for discussion around the lived materialities of folks whose beings serve as sites for the convergence of multiple marginalized identities.

If in contemporary contexts we understand social and political exclusion to refer to the myriad ways select groups are uninvited to wield sociopolitical power, denied access to certain spaces, opportunities, and resources; and relegated to the margins of society, then in this chapter we would like to break tradition to offer the poetic definition of erasure shared below. The following poem was constructed with words extracted from the personal stories about erasure shared with us by Blackwomen and BlackQueer folx close to us. It was our hope to take their words, which represented pain and trauma, and transform them into something beautiful that would recognize the traumas of their lives, but present their lives as something "more than just tragedies" (Boylorn, 2013):

Erasure: A poem

Appropriation

Depreciation

Achievements never celebrated

Actions always already rewarded with

Names never said

Disappeared

Abuse silenced and defended

Left

To die every day

To carry a world that hates you

Invisible

Unremembered

Unexisting

The removal of all traces

If we truly desire to make schools safe and equitable for all students, then we must begin to unearth how certain groups of youth whose bodies are home to multiple marginalized identities do not solely experience exclusion but, further, within *the margins of the margins*, experience erasure. Let us mention that while we recognize our experiences of erasure as different than those of Black heterosexual men, White women, and White queer folks specifically and other groups more generally; we are not interested in participating in the oppression Olympics, where groups vie over 'who has it the hardest.' Simply put, we are lifting up the stories that are often skirted around and not presented in contemporary discourse(s) around educational oppression, discrimination, and exclusion.

We argue that in our bodies and spirits, we carry remnants of the discrimination we have endured due to moments of erasure resulting from racialized sexism and racialized heterosexism. In what follows, we continue in the style of storytelling shared in our opening, as we reflect on moments in our schooling experiences in which we felt invisibilized (read: erased) and instances in which we enjoyed moments of visibility. Afterwards, we expand more on what we mean by the erasure of Blackwomen and BlackQueer folx motivated by racialized (hetero)sexism and connect this phenomenon to the educational experiences of Blackgirls and Black LGBTQ+ youth.

Moments of Erasure

The collision and codeterminative aspects of varying forms of oppression often lead to Blackgirls being vulnerable to abuse, exploitation, dehumanization, and, under the worst circumstances, death. (Morris, 2016, p. 2).

The Blackwoman's body has never truly been acknowledged as her own. It has been the machine from which free labor was reproduced and the object of the master's desire (Gray White, 1999). It has been the source of entertainment, spectacle and seduction put on display for the world's pleasure. It has been the subject of testing and experimentation to advance science and medicine. It has been mocked, mimicked, ridiculed, and appropriated. Her lips have always been too full, her hips too wide, her buttocks too vast, her bosom too voluptuous, her skin too Black, her hair too wooly – all while lip injections, butt and breast implants, tanning and bronzer, and voluminous hair remain desired by the very culture that shuns her. We have seen this over and over again, like when braids, which have been prominent in Black culture for years, are deemed unprofessional for Blackwomen, yet for White women, they become trendy, renamed and claimed, erasing all traces of Blackness in their roots.

The same holds true when Blackwomen are battered, abused and murdered. To be acknowledged, we must create movements like #SayHerName or else risk remaining nameless statistics, unremembered, unworthy of even master's stripping and renaming to which we have grown accustomed. We are then again reminded of our bodies being someone else's to claim when Blackwomen, like Tarana Burke, coin and declare, "me too", yet a decade later, once a White woman claims "#MeToo", it spreads like wildfire and the stories and actions of Blackwomen fade in the background. In recognizing that sexual violence on any person, regardless of race, is unacceptable and hugely problematic, it is also critical to note that the aforementioned historical trauma of the use and abuse of Blackwomen's bodies also means that we experience sexual violence differently than our White female counterparts (Wilson, 2018).

Sexual harassment in schools is commonly experienced by Blackgirls whether educational stakeholders are made privy to it or not. Oftentimes, when reported, it is swept under the rug as, "Boys will be boys" (Crenshaw, Ocen & Nanda, 2015). Other times, Blackgirls suffer silently, abused, exploited, dehumanized, and dying (Morris, 2016). Erased. The following narrative reflects my account (Kat) of this silent suffering:

It was springtime, and warm enough for me (Kat) to wear my favorite blue corduroy hand-me-down dress that, despite its old age, made me feel brand new. It was also the time of year when classmates had already authentically become friends and developed a certain level of comfort with one another. The first graders in MyFirstGradeTeacher's class were antsy and oftentimes rambunctious on days like this, and due to overcrowding at our K–6 elementary school, we were in very close proximity with one another – sharing single-student desks 2:1. MyFirstGradeTeacher, a tall, middle-aged, White woman with shoulder-length dirty-blonde hair, rearranged our seats each week, and that week, I was paired up with ThisFirstGradeBoy. ThisFirstGradeBoy and I were not really friends. In fact, I found him to be quite repulsive.

He was a nose-picker and always made obscene gestures that my six-year-old self didn't quite understand, but never felt good about either. I just knew that spending the week next to ThisFirstGradeBoy was sure to be a nightmare and as it turned out I wasn't wrong. MyFirstGradeTeacher had been trying to gain control of her class of all Black and Brown students ever since she picked us up from our line in the parking lot that morning. Her face was beet red before we had even made it into the classroom. I pitied her because I knew she would have a difficult day but assigning me with ThisFirstGradeBoy meant a difficult day for me too.

He blew kisses at me all through morning roll call and math. I rolled my eyes as hard as I could and tried to focus on my subtraction problems. He attempted to hold my hand throughout all of art. I snatched my fist away and tried to color my picture using the backside of my chair as a support, so my hands could be as far away from him as possible. And then, after MyFirstGradeTeacher raised her voice one too many times, we were made to sit quietly in the dark and read to ourselves. Underneath our shared desk, I felt ThisFirstGradeBoy's left hand gently caress my right knee. Feeling completely disgusted, I quickly slapped it away as hard as I could – so hard that MyFirstGradeTeacher stood up to investigate the sound. She didn't suspect me because I was typically "quiet" and "on task".

I wasn't someone that MyFirstGradeTeacher ever "worried" about. Maybe if I had been, she would've noticed something that was wrong.

ThisFirstGradeBoy's hand made its way to my knee again, and despite my attempts to move him away from me, he persisted. He tried to creep higher and higher up my tiny leg to my thigh, and I knew that repeatedly pushing him away had become ineffective. I decided that my only option was to move myself away from him. I scooted my chair out from under our shared single desk, and into the aisle I went. MyFirstGradeTeacher looked up at me when she heard the commotion of my heavy chair dragging across the floor. She called my name from across the classroom sternly. Everyone looked my way. She commanded me to put my chair back under my desk. I felt embarrassed. I felt alone. In a room full of people, where everyone stared right at me, no one saw me. ThisFirstGradeBoy snickered knowing that he had won. I didn't move. I was frozen. I didn't want to go back. I was being tormented and she hadn't even noticed. I mustered out one simple word, "But..." and was silenced by MyFirstGradeTeacher's demanding, "Now!"

She didn't really see me. She didn't even really try to. Somehow, between morning roll call and that very moment, I had been erased. I knew, then, I was invisible. My six-year-old self didn't quite understand that invisibility back then, but I never felt good about either. The pain in my chest became sharp and immediate. I knew this would do lasting damage. That's when I died for the very first time. Left. Invisible. Unexisting. Lost.

> Navigating the intersectionality of race, gender, class, spirituality, and sexual orientation has been like playing an endless game of chess. (Hucks, 2017, p. 126)

I (Shamari) am not sure who said it first but growing up I heard repeatedly that the Blackwomen in my life "couldn't win for losing." As a youth, I may not have been ready to understand what exactly was to be communicated with such a phrase, but the older I got and the more I embraced my BlackQueer identity, the closer I got to its meaning. No matter what I did or where I moved, there were always racist or heterosexist landmines ready to claim my body. Don't be too Black. Don't be too Gay. Any wrong move could position my BlackQueer body in a new line of attack. It was like an endless game of chess. A game I couldn't win for losing.

Fortunately, I am unable to draw upon moments in my life in which I was bullied, heckled, or made to feel physically unsafe at school because of my misunderstood BlackQueer identity. Those things weren't possible for me because I stopped going to school in kindergarten. I mean, someone occupying my body attended school, but I never went. Every day as I got ready, I would put on the appropriate school attire and take off myself. I would leave myself at home. There was no place for me at school. I was a BlackQueer cisgender boy who learned very early on that self-preservation was synonymous with self-erasure. Like my co-author, who accounts in the above narratives, I too had internalized this erasure. I performed erasure. I gave my peers and teachers (and society) who they wanted: A straight Black boy, who wasn't smart, who didn't like math, who was really good at sports, who hated playing with dolls, who couldn't read, who lagged behind his White peers in standardized test scores because of an illusory achievement gap, who didn't love other boys, but who loved to entertain. That was my role. If I kept them laughing, they wouldn't ask questions – questions about "my type," or my girlfriend, or my hobbies, or what I thought of last night's game.

We were sitting on the rug. My best friend, Derrick, and I were there in the back, hidden behind all the other *normal* children. Because it was unacceptable not to, and due to the obsession with controlling the Black body, I somehow managed to keep my legs crossed and my eyes on the speaker during the entirety of storytime. My teacher was not an excellent storyteller, but my Black imagination was dope, so I looked forward to storytime. It was an invitation to be present, even if only in my own mind. The teacher was to tell a story about a family. A word that I had to come to define based on my own experiences and interactions with aunts, sisters, girl cousins, mothers, and other mothers. Family, for me, was Blackwomen. The teacher asked for our assistance. "So, let's imagine we have a family, starting with the parents. We have a mom and a dad. What should their names be?" I was only four feet tall, weighed no more than 50 pounds and had only been around for 60 or so full moons, but even I knew that not all families needed a mother and a father. Some families just needed a mother, sisters, girl cousins, and an aunt; while others just needed queer love. My classmates, including Derrick, threw out names. Ultimately, the teacher went with Barbara and Dave. That was a family. Two parents. A mother. A father. And children. Anything else would not constitute family in this narrative.

School was the place where we were supposed to co-construct knowledge about life, death, and everything in between. As students, we were to trust that our teacher would guide us to discover the most important lessons of life. I am not sure what the lesson to be taught was that day, but I learned one that I have been trying to unlearn for over 20 years. Families with two same-sex parents were not possible; Families without fathers were broken. Families flowing from queer love were not imaginable. That day, my teacher taught me that my current family comprised of strong Blackwomen, absent Black cisgender men, was not a family, and queer love would never be enough to raise a child. Erasure. That was the last day I went to school.

Moments of Visibility

Too often BlackQueer folx and Blackwomen are forced to assimilate and conform to dominant cultural norms in order to be regarded as human; in order to be seen (Bruce, 2016; Johnson, 2016; Story, 2016). However, that process of assimilation always comes at a cost. Though we may be afforded temporary conditional sociocultural acceptance if we perform our sexual, racial, and gender identities in ways that do not disrupt the White supremacist patriarchy, it often comes at the expense of ourselves (Bruce, 2016; Love, 2017; Story, 2016). This "fitting in" too frequently requires that we engage in the constant policing of our bodies and the ways we move through life in them. Thus, aided by society, we unconsciously perform self-erasure. And these seemingly innocuous invitations to "fit in" or risk rejection, bullying, or harassment, have deleterious effects on Blackgirls and BlackQueer youth in schools (Pritchard, 2013; Crenshaw, Ocen & Nanda, 2015). For example, many studies have revealed with striking clarity how Blackgirls and BlackQueer youth who feel unable to embrace their identities in school, often recount educational experiences marked by harassment, violence, isolation, depression, truancy, and low levels of self-esteem (Brockenbrough, 2016; Pritchard, 2013; Crenshaw, Ocen, & Nanda, 2015).

In addition, when youth from these groups seek support from school communities, they are often met with further harassment and discrimination from school staff or their claims are ignored (Bridges, 2007). It is important to reflect on these experiences and moments of invisibility, as we seek to analyze our educational homes and the messages we send to our most marginalized students about their self-worth and racialized, sexualized, and gendered identities. It is also worth mentioning that some BlackQueers and Blackwomen after realizing the inability or unwillingness of schools to visiblize them, reject common sense notions of who we are supposed to be and affirm ourselves and others who share similar social identity markers (Love, 2017). In other words, we learn to love who we are and others like us. And we visiblize ourselves and each other. The narratives below speak to these moments of visibilization.

Whether you're transgender or not, most of us get to a point in our lives where we can no longer lie to ourselves; We are not what other people say we are. We are who we know ourselves to be, and we are what we love. (Laverne Cox quoted in; Rueckert, 2017)

Shamari: It was a conversation between ghosts. It was because of this conversation that I begin to peel away all the layers of personified stereotypes of the (heterosexual) Black boy and unlearn all my lines for a play called *The Erasure of the BlackQueer*. I was 13 when I met her. Her name was Aya. She was a Blackgirl. Aya and I had been friends for about a year and I thought things were going well. We would spend all day in school together and all night on the phone saying the things we were never invited to share in our classes. But one day Aya revealed to me that she thought our friendship was one-sided. She expressed that she had no idea who I was. She spoke of how she had revealed so much to me about her life as a Blackgirl, but all I ever did was listen. I never reciprocated. She made it very clear that though she would join me in the background during the school day, she would visiblize herself during our private phone conversations. In other words, she would embrace her identity. Unlike in school, during our phone conversations she would no longer hide behind empty words and half-truths about who she was and what she could become. However, she was aware that I chose to remain invisible; she was unhappy. Our friendship was uneven. The next day, I wrote Aya an email in which I told her I was gay. She called me and I could hear the excitement in her voice because finally there would be someone on the other side of the call – an interlocutor: A listener. Someone who would share their opinions and ideas. I was visible. She could see me. She could love me. And she did. Our conversations would no longer be those between ghosts. Whenever we were together, we would both be present.

From our earliest years, Blackwomen draw strength and inspiration from our heritage and the women who came before us. We learn from them how to be okay, even when the world seems mad. (Harris, 2015, p. 122)

Kat: Between kindergarten and 12th grade, I had more than 30 different teachers, only three of whom were Blackwomen. In fact, while Blackgirls make up 16% of America's student population, 80% of our teachers are White, while 7% of teachers and 10% of principals are Black (US Department of Education, 2016). This disproportionate representation of Black teachers and principals creates a slim chance for Blackgirls to encounter Blackwomen as their teachers or school leaders and leaves ample room for them to be misread, misunderstood, excluded and erased.

The interactions between Blackwomen can serve as sources of strength and inspiration (Harris, 2015). When Blackgirls are forced to navigate school and society, where they face constant exclusion and rebuke, the role that Blackwomen can play in their sustainment and healing is unparalleled. Education stakeholders must make greater efforts to actively recruit Black teachers to obtain a more realistic reflection of society, cater to the needs of the students they serve, and ensure that the students in the margins of the margins do not go unseen. The following narrative depicts my experience with loss and the ways in which a Blackwoman teacher visibilized and validated me in my time of grief.

* * *

In fifth grade, my teacher died in the middle of the school year at the age of 32. He had a stroke and was found on the floor of his home over the weekend. That Monday morning, the phone rang right before it was time for me to get in the shower. Before my mama even picked up, I knew something was wrong. She called me into the living room and uttered the words, "Mr. Williams passed away." I stared blankly unsure of what I should say and unable to say anything whether or not words came to mind. She followed with, "Are you ok?" I shrugged my shoulders trying to give off the impression that I was fine. Why didn't I want my mama to know I wasn't? She knew anyway. She didn't need me to say the words. I turned and walked out of the living room to carry on business as usual, entering into the bathroom, closing the door behind me, and turning on the shower water. I stepped in and fell to the floor as if my knees gave out just in time for me to be perfectly alone. I cried and cried for what felt like forever. Then I picked myself up, and began scrubbing the pain away.

I went to school that morning ready to just get by. They announced Mr. Williams' death in the cafeteria that morning and my classmates and I held each other tightly in small circles as we cried together. No one else seemed to be affected. Only our class. Since sixth grade had been transferred to middle school, we were the eldest students in the building, and the only ones who would've have really had a relationship with Mr. Williams, who taught fifth grade for longer than I could remember.

After the announcement, everyone went off to their respective classrooms, ours was located outside in a trailer near the school building due to the overcrowding. After a few minutes passed, our principal, a round White man who stuck out like a sore thumb in our neighborhood, came in and said, "If anyone needs to see the grief counselors, please let your sub know. They'll be here all day." And then he walked out. A room full of 10-11-year-olds, left with a sub they had never even seen before to figure out what grief counseling was and whether or not they needed it.

Soon after, the door opened again. This time, it was a child. A small fourth-grader toting a folded piece of paper walked up to our substitute and handed it off. The sub read the note, and called out my name: "Cathryn, Ms. Brown wants to see you." Ms. Brown was my fourth-grade teacher, and the first teacher I ever loved. She was a young Blackwoman, who understood being a young Blackgirl because she once was. When I opened the door of Ms. Brown's classroom, she didn't say a word. Instead she spread her arms out wide summoning me into her embrace. I ran to her full speed crashing right into her arms giving my tears permission to flow freely. With a class full of students sitting at desks silently, Ms. Brown carved a special space just for me. And out of the 41 students in her class when I was a fourth-grader, it was only me who she summoned. It was me who she remembered. It was me who she saw. Words we didn't need. All we needed was each other.

> What a miracle it is that despite everything we are taught we dare to love ourselves and each other. (Alexis Pauline Gumbs, cited in Pritchard, 2017, p.192)

* * *

Kat: As I began to reflect on my past journey through Blackgirlhood and current journey of Blackwomanhood, I realized that at times when I felt most visible, it was at the hands (or in the arms) of a Blackwoman. Whether at my lowest point bringing me back to life or at my highest point upholding me on her shoulders, Blackwomen have spoken back to my erasure, made room at the table for me and reminded me that even when I can't see myself, they see me. Blackwomen have the ability to save other Blackwomen and girls like no one else because they know the walk and the ways. They have read and written the untold stories. They need no explanation.

Shamari: I have always felt connected to Blackwomen, too. I feel something in them. I feel radical revolutionary Black love that affirms and visiblizes me. That holds me. That protects me. And invites me to love back. That welcomes my BlackQueer love with open souls. Our experiences are not the same, but they aren't entirely different either. We aren't heterosexual cisgender Black men and we aren't White women or White queer folks. To them, we're ghosts. But together, symbiotically, we are able to exist in two places at once, phase through buildings, worlds, and hearts, and leverage our translucence to sit back ensconced in the shadows of the margins and watch the world turn, undisturbed. Watch the world turn because of us, unrewarded.

Kat: We carry the world on our backs and know that feeling of when the world doesn't say thank you for it.

Shamari: We know how to be mothers when needed, friends when requested, confidants when sought out, motivators when it feels right, and sisters all the time.

Kat: We know endurance through pain and we've mastered the art of making something out of nothing because sitting with nothing can never be an option.

Shamari: "We know how to throw shade on normativity, sashay away from a politics of respectability, and get our lives from a politics of deviance" (Story, 2016, p.364).

Kat: We are fine as wine created from water, nourishing the souls of the deserving and the undeserving. We see needs unseen and fill voids unfillable. We know when the light leaves a Blackgirl's eyes, and how to light it up again.

Shamari: We play every role that matters.

Kat: We are superheroes, warriors, and soldiers – and we save, war and fight with love and grace.

Shamari: We know the youth are watching. The youth are listening. They are desperately looking for themselves in books, on the big screens, and in the stories we tell to and about them. And somewhere, if we aren't careful, a little Blackgirl and her best friend, a little Blackgay boy are being disappeared. Erased.

Kat: And so, we must move away from single-identity narratives of exclusion so that greater variations of the Black experience, the Queer experience, the Woman experience, and experiences of oppression become available. Experiences like ours become visible, thus, we become visiblized.

Kat & Shamari: And we can write ourselves and other BlackQueer folx, Blackwomen, and other multiply oppressed groups back into the U.S. American story.

Erasure of Blackwomen/Blackqueer Folx

It is worth repeating that the narrative accounts relayed above should not be generalized and made to speak to all of the embodied realities of discrimination of all Blackgirls and BlackQueer youth, as Love (2017) cautions in her piece on the Black ratchet imagination. Though our narratives may diverge at many points, at the heart of them is the shared understanding of erasure. Invisibility. If we accept that many groups, due to their social identity markers, have been excluded, then we must simultaneously recognize that Blackwomen and BlackQueer folx, due to the pervasiveness of racialized sexism and racialized heterosexism, often find themselves inhabiting the margins of the margins – spaces that can be characterized as sociopolitical spaces that are excluded even within markers of difference such as Black personhood and Queer identity.

One example of this intersectionality (Crenshaw, 1989), in terms of disciplinary focus, comes about when feminist theory and queer theory fail to include the experiences of Blackwomen and BlackQueer folx on a theoretical and pragmatic level (Cohen, 2004). Concurrently, on an interpersonal level, many folks operationalize these theories touting the White woman's experience is representative of all women, consequently moving some White women to conflate the experiences of Blackwomen and White women in an attempt to claim solidarity (Reed, 2016). Similarly, the White LGBTQ+ community rarely entertains the idea that BlackQueers may experience the world differently than them due to our racialized/sexualized identities (Ellison, 2016). The same could be said about equating the experiences of Black men and Blackwomen (Griffin, Bennett, & Harris, 2013).

In conflating the experiences, specifically in the instances with White women, White queer folks, and Black heterosexual men, this misunderstanding of the multiple marginalization faced by those of us who have been forcibly denied visibility allows those who may benefit from heterosexual and racial/gender privilege (as in the above examples) to disavow their privilege and ignore the many ways they contribute to our oppression. That is, when White women claim to experience gender oppression just as Blackwomen do, they neglect to question their unearned racial privilege; the same is true for White LGBTQ+ people who often proudly proclaim that love is love but that all lives matter (Reed, 2016). This blatant disregard for the unique and precarious situations in which Blackwomen and BlackQueer folx live is dangerous, as it leaves us alone to fend for ourselves as we navigate sticky social terrain littered with racist, sexist, and heterosexist landmines.

This erasure of and disregard for our experiences becomes patently obvious when we begin to examine the experiences of Blackgirls and BlackQueer youth. For example, when speaking of the school-to-prison pipeline, only recently (and quite minimally) has the conversation been extended to include how Blackgirls are pushed out of schools and into the carceral apparatus and suffer disproportionately at the hands of gender violence. Similarly, there are even fewer studies that explore how Black LGBTQ+ students are pushed out of schools due to their unwillingness or inability to conform to dominant heteronorms (McCready, 2004). Indeed, though some education scholars have recently begun to examine the experiences of LGBTQ+ youth of color, research and public dialogue around how LGBTQ+ people of color make up 73% of anti-LGBTQ+ hate crimes and of which almost 54% are Blackqueers is wanting (Ellis, 2016).

Additionally, the latest GLSEN (Gay, Lesbian & Straight Education Network) climate survey, revealed that 22% of all BlackQueer youth feel unsafe in schools and 53.4% of BlackQueer youth reported anti-LGBTQ+ discrimination. In this same survey, we also learn when compared to their White counterparts, Black LGBTQ+ youth are more likely to experience suicidal thoughts, depression, homelessness, and physical violence in schools. Bridges (2007) also found that LGBTQ+ students of color who experience high severities of harassment based on both their sexual and racial identities have significantly lower grade point averages than students who report experiencing a high severity of harassment because of only one of these identities. And students of color who are severely harassed in school because of both their sexual identity and race are more likely to miss school than those who are severely harassed based on sexual identity or race only (Bridges, 2007). Nonetheless, attention to the specific experiences of these groups is lacking and their experiences never find their way into discourse on LGBTQ+ and Black youth (Pritchard, 2003).

Conclusive Remarks

In this chapter, we have made the conscious decision to decenter and silence dominant narratives so that the positionalities of BlackQueers and Blackwomen take center stage. Each and every word in this chapter has been handpicked from and created by Blackwomen and BlackQueer folx as a payment of homage to our roles as experts of our own lives and holders of valuable knowledge. In doing so, we maintain that if we acknowledge and honor these, our unique perspectives, we may find ourselves closer to achieving the seemingly elusive goal of providing all students with an equitable education, and answering the calls of Blackwomen and BlackQueer folx when they cry out:

Where is our space? Where do we seek refuge? Where is the acknowledgement of those of us who are not Black on Monday, Queer on Tuesday, Woman on Thursday, but BlackQueer, Blackwoman, and BlackQueerWoman every day? Why won't you say our names? Where is our appreciation? Why aren't we commemorated? Why can't you see us?

REFERENCES

Boylorn, R.M. (2013). *Sweetwater: Black women and narratives of resilience.* New York, NY: Peter Lang.

Bridges, E. (2007). "Advocates for youth report on the impact of homophobia and racism on GLBTQ youth of color". Retrieved from: http://www.advocatesforyouth.org/publications/publications-a-z/425-the-impact-of-homophobia-and-racism-on-glbtq-youth-of-color

Brockenbrough, E. (2016). Becoming queerly responsive: Culturally responsive pedagogy for Black and latino urban queer youth. *Urban Education, 51,* 170- 196.

Bruce, L.J. (2016). The body beautiful: Black drag, American cinema, and heteroperpetually ever after. In E.P. Johnson (Ed.), *No tea, no shade: New writings in Black queer studies* (pp.166-195). Durham: Duke University Press.

Cohen, C. J. (2004). Deviance as resistance: A new research agenda for the study of Black politics. *Du Bois Review, 1*(1), 27-45.

Crenshaw, K (1989) Demarginalizing the intersection of race and sex: A Black feminist critique of antidiscrimination doctrine, feminist theory and antiracist politics. *University of Chicago Legal Forum* 139–167.

Crenshaw K. W., Ocen, P., & Nanda, J. (2015). *Black girls matter: Pushed out, overpoliced and underprotected.* New York: African American Policy Forum.

Davis, C. (2017). From Colorism to Conjurings: Tracing the Dust in Beyoncé's Lemonade. *Taboo: The Journal of Culture & Education, 16*(2), 7–28.

Ellison, T.(2016). The strangeness of progress and the uncertainty of Blackness. In E.P. Johnson (ed.), *No tea, no shade: New writings in Black queer studies* (pp.48-64). Durham: Duke University Press.

Gray White, D. (1999). Ar'n't I a Woman?: Female slaves in the plantation south. New York: Norton.

Griffin, K.A., Bennett, J.C., & Harris, J. (2013). Marginalizing merit?: Gender differences in Black faculty D/discourses on tenure, advancement, and professional success. *Review of Higher Education, 36,* 489-512.

Harris, T. W. (2015). *The sisters are alright: Changing the broken narrative of Black women in America.* Oakland, CA: Berrett-Koehler Publishers, Inc.

Hines-Datiri, D & Carter Andrews, D. J. (2017). The effects of zero tolerance policies on Black girls: Using critical race feminism and figured worlds to examine school discipline. *Urban Education, 122.*

Hucks, D. (2017). Intersectional warrior: Battling the onslaught of layered microaggressions in the academy. In S.J. Miller, & N. M. Rodriguez (eds.), *Educators queering academia: Critical memoirs* (pp.125-135). New York, NY: Peter Lang.

Johnson, E.P. (2016). Introduction. In *No tea, no shade: New writings in Black queer studies* (pp.1-26). Durham: Duke University Press.

Lorde, A. (2007). Sister outsider. Berkeley, CA: Crossing. (Original work published in 1984).

Love, B.T. (2017). A ratchet lens: Black queer youth, agency, hip hop, and the Black ratchet imagination. *Educational Researcher, 46,* 539-547.

McCready, L.T. (2004). Understanding the marginalization of gay and gender -onconforming Black male students. *Theory Intro Practice, 43,* 136-143

Morris, M. W. (2016). *Pushout: The criminalization of Black girls in schools.* New York: The New Press.

Pritchard, E. D. (2013). For colored kids who committed suicide, our outrage isn't enough: Queer youth of color, bullying, and the discursive limits of identity and safety. *Harvard Educational Review, 83,* 320-345.

Pritchard, E. D. (2017). *Fashioning lives: Black queers and the politics of literacy.* SIU Press.

Reed, A. (2016). The Whiter the bread, the quicker you're dead: Spectacular absence and post-racialized Blackness in (White) queer theory. In E.P. Johnson (ed.), *No tea, no shade: New writings in Black queer studies* (pp.324-345). Durham: Duke University Press.

Rueckert, P. (2017, May). 33 quotes that show Laverne Cox just gets it. *Global Citizen.* Online.

Retrieved from: https://www.globalcitizen.org/en/content/laverne-cox-birthday-quotes/

Story, K.A. (2016). On the cups of deviance: Respectability politics and the cultural marketplace of sameness. In E.P. Johnson (ed.), *No tea, no shade: New writings in Black queer studies* (pp.362-379). Durham: Duke University Press.

Wilson, Y. (2018). Why Black women's experiences of #MeToo are different. *The Conversation*. Retrieved from: https://theconversation.com/why-Black-womens-experiences-of-metoo-are-different-96091.

Chapter 5

THESE VIOLENT [~~DELIGHTS~~] HAVE VIOLENT ENDS

Rising Up, Pushing Back, and the Possibility of Hope

Emily A. Nusbaum, Danielle Cowley, David Hernández-Saca, Amy Peterson & Phil Smith

"The wound is the place where the light enters you" – Rumi

The group of narratives in this chapter represent the structural, institutional, political, material, and personal violence of the traditional canon and system of special education, from a range of positions and relational spaces. We argue that this violence is an extension of the ongoing exclusion and erasure of disability from most educational contexts *except* special education and associated fields, which have historically promoted, and have currently become, systems of violence in relation to the lived realities of students and adults labeled with disabilities – including professionals working within teacher education.

Our stories come together in this chapter from diverse identities and experiences – some of us claim a disabled identity, some of us experience impairment but are able to "pass." Some of us also have been labeled with a disability in K–12 education, while others are parents of K–12 children who are labeled with disabilities. However, all of us navigate the in/between and tenuous spaces of Disability Studies in Education (DSE) as an (inter)disciplinary framework, as well as a philosophical, conceptual, and pragmatic approach to education.

P.A. Boda (ed.), Essays on Exclusion, 85–109.

These spaces are neither fully immersed in special education, nor do they equate entirely to other disciplines that may take up disability as a form of difference for accommodation and assimilation. Our situated ways of making sense of disability and exclusion are also neither accepted within social justice in education discourses nor held within the dominant, deficit discourse of special education. In this way, the narratives we present here attempt to subvert myopic views toward disability and challenge the readers to think about how new narrations of disability can shape and shade a goal toward equity in education that emphasizes inclusion rather than perpetuating exclusion. Before we embark on our collective journey, though, we must situate our own narratives within the larger field of DSE, as well as be transparent about our individuated approaches.

Disability Studies in Education:
A Background on Our Use of the Term

Disability Studies in Education (DSE), as we define it and operationalize it here in our analyses, is a distinctly different venture than traditional special education. We recognize the need to scrutinize ideas about disability that are conveyed in K–12 education, policy and practice, as well as reified in higher education. The rationale for this project should be recognized as distinct from the typical P–12 concerns regarding disability that all too often fall within the "exclusive purview of special education," (Ware, 2017) and within the realm of legislation, such as the Americans with Disabilities Act (ADA; 1990) or the Individuals with Disabilities Education Act (IDEA; 2004). In the absence of understanding disability as a welcome aspect of society in higher education institutions and P–12 education, we argue, instead, for a recognition of the limits of current thinking about disability as devalued humanity.

DSE, thus, positions disability as something socially and culturally constructed – an identity that intersects with and is co-constructed with other social markers, such as race/ethnicity, gender identity, geography, and socioeconomic status (Annamma, Ferri, & Connor, 2018; Hernández-Saca, Kahn, & Cannon, 2018). Within a DSE paradigm, "disability" is created in P–12 schooling as students come into contact with normative practices and structures, inaccessible pedagogy and curriculum, as well as educational legislation and policies that position deficit-based labels as useful, and which mandate their use in order for a student to receive supports and services that are deemed to be "special." Given this, we now turn to elaborate on our own narratives that brought us to take up this particular paradigm and how it connects to exclusion in education.

Purpose

There are many possible explanations for the forms of exclusion connected to disability across educational landscapes. Some of these explanations are tied to the enduring power of the positivist paradigm (and associated theory, research, and practice), which frames disability as an inherent deficit in the individual body/mind (Heshusius & Ballard, 1996). This positivist paradigm, which is the foundation of traditional special education, relies on "ways of knowing" (Gallagher, 2004; Ware, 2002) about disability and is firmly entrenched in essentialist and individually applied deficit-based characteristics that identify disability (broadly) as deviation from some kind of idealized norm (Dudley-Marling & Gurn, 2010). Also understood as the individual model of disability, this deficit model places "disability" as something that can be identified (and thus remediated, fixed, or intervened upon) in an individual.

This limited (and dangerous) understanding of disability results in multiple forms of exclusion that range from personal to epistemic, extending from the fear and discomfort about a social identity shaped primarily by deficit and pathology that has resulted in a limited and limiting understanding of disability as a valued identity and way of being in the world. This lack of "disability literacy" (reading/knowing/understanding disability) (Dickens, Reamy, Nusbaum, 2015) beyond these deficit-based ways of knowing results in holding fast to the notion of false binaries that mark some body/minds as distinctly regular/special or disabled/normal. We see this exemplified at multiple levels – from the division between general and special education departments and programs at universities, the separation of faculty and students within these programs, the existence of different national standards for those teaching students marked as "regular" or "special," and the relegation of disability to the disability services closet at institutions of higher education.

We build this chapter from a previous conference workshop that we developed collectively and will share stories that represent our individual experiences with educational exclusion. In turn, we illuminate the forms of ableism and personally experienced structural, relational, and institutional violence from the traditional canon and system of special education across K–12 and higher education contexts. Our collective voice defines this kind of exclusion as very active, as well as through insidious forms of passive resistance and refusal. Throughout the chapter, we envision a reprieve from the ongoing violence we currently encounter and move towards the realization of plurality, equity, and recognition of a collective humanity that includes all body/minds. We believe that bearing witness to our stories, which capitalize on our diverse positions and relational spaces, has the possibility of a form of critical praxis – critical reflection and action (Artiles & Kozleski, 2007) – that bridges theory and practice, possibly re-shaping the road toward equity in education.

Narrating Exclusion

The four stories shared here use a range of narrative strategies and visual representation to articulate experiences of educational exclusion and disability. Emily uses Heshusius's (1989) concept of "paradigm a metaphor" to try and understand the very active forms of institutional violence and ongoing passive forms of resistance and refusal the have occurred across her institutional experiences. David uses narrative and imagery to unpack his identity and experiences as a dis/abled high school student in the process of identity reclamation. Amy and Danielle use text messages to highlight the metaphor of their professional reflection practices as existing in "cracks" and through metaphor they also extend their work into special education/teacher education, trying to "do" DSE as it relates to their personal experience in the field and academia. Finally, Phil shares his experience in and outside a school of education on his university campus and highlights his ongoing exclusion in attempting to "do" disability studies within this context. As we present our narratives about exclusion, we encourage readers to consider their own experiences with, perhaps, more visible forms exclusion such as interpersonal and structural micro-aggressions that along race, gender, sexual orientation, or other lines within educational contexts and other professional settings; power issues as it relates to institutional decisions spanning the classroom, school, and school district, among others that are related to your particular positionalities within the system of public education.

Emily: Educational Exclusion

To describe exclusion is so deeply personal and almost always painful if shared honestly – and yet, it needs to be named. I have come to find the metaphor of the ocean as useful to understand my own experiences of exclusion in education. There are places and moments when the water is calm and I can relax, walk in slowly and with ease, and lie back and float, unworried and with peace. There are also times when, wading out into the water, a big wave rises unexpectedly with force, and knocks me down – scraping my body on the rough sand, rocks, and shells below, standing up and being knocked down again. Sometimes this exclusion feels like being out in deep water that is so blue and dark that I cannot see anything below me, trying to manage the fear about the danger that is possibly there. With inevitability, like the tides, I know that the fear of being knocked, scraped, and pulled under will always happen. And that again, I might need to retreat and wait for the water and waves to recede. In this way of placing metaphor to the exclusion I have experienced, I share some of my experiences with both active and enduring forms of exclusion within spaces of traditional special education, and also those experiences that might be described as more passive forms of resistance and refusal, which seem to erase both me and the critical content related to disability that is at the core of what I teach and write about.

Heshusius's (1989) concept "paradigm-as-metaphor" is useful in supporting an understanding of the distinct divide between me, and my thinking, writing, and teaching- ultimately who I am – from many of the colleagues in traditional special education departments where I have worked and from my colleagues outside of special education who cannot place disability within diversity and justice in education frameworks. "Paradigm-as-metaphor" refers to the ways in which we view, understand, and experience the world- and as such is a metaphor that allows me, in the moments where I am knocked down by a huge wave, or waiting in fear in deep, dark blue water, to understand why these spaces of exclusion exist. Ways of knowing about disability that emerge within disability studies and all its subfields position disability (the disabled bodymind) as a natural part of human variation – versus as a liability or as something to be "cured" or "fixed." Yet, within schools of education disability, has and largely remains, the distinct purview of special education – as something to be intervened on or managed, in the pursuit of an idealized "normal."

This concept is also useful to understand my experiences teaching many pre/early-service special education teachers, many of whom have formed a distinct identity of their relationship to disabled students based on traditional, positivist frameworks. My teaching commitments to both the ideology of inclusive education, as well as the tenets of critical disability studies requires these teachers to scrutinize received ideas about disability that are conveyed in K–12 education, as well as within teacher education, which exist to the detriment of more fully understanding disability and the response to disability within K-12 education as a social justice issue. These commitments push teachers that I teach – many of whom are not necessarily willing participants – to the edges of their own paradigms.

For example, I frequently teach a course on collaboration with families, students, and other education professionals in special education/teacher education. I teach this course through both applied/practical content (such as: working effectively with instructional aides, co-teaching, and utilizing a transdisciplinary approach), as well as framed through a practice of critical reflection on power and ways that power dynamics are exercised between education professionals and families/students labeled with disability. Although these liminal spaces provide the possibility for deep transformation of the self (within my students), they also represent my teaching, and my being in the classroom, spaces of fear and the possibility of being knocked down again.

This is most evident in the comments on teaching evaluations – comments that equate my content with opinion ("Emily has strong opinions and doesn't let us have our own ideas about teaching and inclusion"), comments that indicate the deep discomfort with reflecting on power and power differentials between school professionals and families ("Emily made us feel bad in this class"), and comments that indicate the need to hold tightly to essentialist ways-of-knowing about students labeled with disability ("Emily kept talking about how to be good advocates, and what I want to know is what students with autism are like"). When coupled with low numeric scores on these teaching evaluations, I am left fearful and alone, in deep, dark blue water.

"You disability people are always worried about access" repeated by a colleague, with a smile and a joking tone, each time I bring up issues of accessibility in various meetings. Comments like these and the silences that happen around disability in schools of education should be expected by now, I know and tell myself repeatedly. But both feel like being pulled down by a big wave and thrown against the bottom of the ocean – I can stand up and sputter and prepare myself for it to happen again, all the time knowing that cost for my own emotional being and feeling safe within the place where I am supposed to go to work each day. "How many times should I mention it?" I ask myself silently, in professional conversations where the topic is focused on identifying spaces of critical commitment or ways to enhance faculty collaborations related to educational issues. In these moments I am the deep, dark water of the ocean- not knowing what is underneath. Perhaps I hope it will be different, although this hope is, at best, naïve. There is silence that ensues. And so I wait and speak up again and point out who isn't present in our current dialogue (students labeled with disability). And again, silence. Sometimes my energy is good and I have the capacity to point out how *disability is about and for all of us.* And more often than not, after three or four tries, I sit quietly, take off my glasses so that I cannot really see anyone clearly anymore, and tell myself over and over that my work, my perspectives, and my contributions *do matter.* Even when ignored – more so refused – in spaces committed to generative dialogue about critical issues and justice in education.

My presence in educational spaces that claim a justice identity, and that also continue to relegate discussions of disability to the pathologizing paradigms of special education represents, perhaps, the edges of a justice paradigm that have erased the very being of the disabled bodymind. Although I still struggle to make sense of a profession that marginalizes the very people it claims to serve (i.e., special education) – and more so am, Heshusius' writing about "paradigm-as-metaphor" has at least given me words through which to identify the source of this oppression that thus extends even to me.

David: Taking the S.A.T. While Labeled LD: The Importance of Student Voice and Emotionality for Healing

What does it feel like to be a student labeled with an auditory Learning Disability and take the S.A.T.? For me, it felt humiliating, embarrassing, shameful and a loss of dignity. In this way, I use Disability Studies in Education (DSE) and radical love (Fromm, 1956) to make sense of one of my Learning Disability (LD) oppression moments to explore this question. DSE provides me with theoretical tools, such as the social-psycho-emotional model of disability (Hernández-Saca & Cannon, 2016; Thomas, 1999) to heal and to use an alternative framework toward the meanings of disability rather than those institutionalized within the field of LD, special education and broader society.

Thomas (1999) defines social-psycho-emotional disablism as "a form of social oppression involving the social imposition of restrictions of activity on people with impairments and the socially engendered undermining of their psycho-emotional well-being" (p. 604). Radical love (Fromm, 1956) provides me with a mind-heart framework to move forward given my negative experiences with LD and special education. In particular, the virtues and values of "care, responsibility, respect, and knowledge" (Fromm, 1956, p. 24) for myself and others within society can mediate the past, present and future violence that systems of power at the epistemological, ontological, axiological and etiological levels, such as the field of LD and special education has had and can have on the lived experiences of disabled students.

In other words, the combination of DSE and radial love informs my critical emotion praxis (Zembylas, 2015) as it relates to my experiences and understandings of what it means to be labeled with LD and having been in special education. My critical emotion praxis of my LD pain, emotions and trauma can lead towards reconciliation and healing by finding my academic voice and processing my negative LD emotionality.

Below I present a critical autoethnographic vignette (Foley, 2002; Humphreys, 2005) about my experience taking the S.A.T. in high school. The vignette includes my autoethnographic interpretations about a series of paintings I did to process this LD and special education oppressive experience. My autoethnographic paintings started with the tattoo I got on my chest when I was in graduate school at a point when I was exhausted and tired of suffering about "my LD" (See Figure 1). It's a quote from Buddha that reminds me to self-love and love to transcend the damage imagery that has dominated my mind and soul regarding my LD and special education experiences.

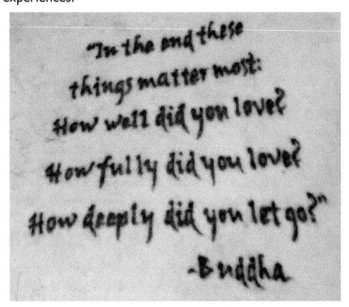

Figure 1. David's Buddha tattoo.

I painted the first part of the tattoo on the first canvas presented as in Figure 2 on the next page. I decided to not write the last part of the tattoo on canvas #1 but represent it as the last canvas in a different form than the original text (see Figure 6). The original text was: *How deeply did you let go?*

The second and third canvas (see Figure 3 and 4) represents an institutional disability micro- aggression I experienced during high school when I went to take my S.A.T. exam at the neighborhood high school. The high school color was green and that is why I chose a green background on the canvas.

Figure 2. David's Canvas #1: "In the end."

Figure 3. David's Canvas #2: "S.A.T. 'Special Education'"

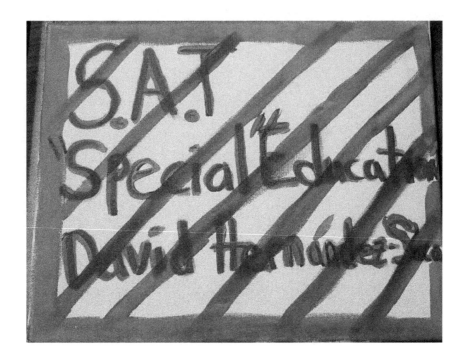

Figure 4. David's Canvas #3: "Lines across 'S.A.T.'"

I choose red, however, for the writing since when I was walking to take my S.A.T. exam I noticed a huge sign that read, "S.A.T. Special Education, David Hernandez-Saca →" When I first saw the sign, I immediately felt this rush of embarrassment and shame overtake my body and spirit. This experience has always stuck with me as a time that I experienced shameful "LD emotions" (Hernández-Saca, 2016) but never had a chance to express how I felt and the humiliation and powerlessness I felt and continue to feel. This visual representation of my 'LD' and 'special education' labels within a formal academic space embodied the way I felt. The sign literally threw me into a psychological-emotional and social prison as it related to my academic sense of self that I stored away in my mind, body and spirit. I felt as those I was under surveillance and watched; and the invalidation of my freedom and sense of value to myself as it related to being a student. In retrospect, I was never asked how I wanted to be included or "accommodated" or the ways the meanings of special education were constructed for "me." In the end, who benefited from such an arrangement?

The fourth painting (Figure 5) represents my journey toward healing because when I painted this canvas my partner shared with me that the colors, within the Navajo culture, represent those of a medicine man. When he told me that, I immediately felt new in my spirit and soul. I also felt that I needed to continue to paint and write about my experiences with LD and special education as a way towards healing, reaffirming that I am not alone and neither are others that may have shared experiences. Painting allowed me to be free. Painting allowed me to be mad at my LD and special education experiences to understand my academic self, and not be lost in my pain and hurt that my associations of being labeled with LD have created inside of me. From a DSE approach, understanding the phenomenology of those living with disabilities is of paramount significance in order to have a window into the life-world of feeling and experiencing disability that is personal, structural and political. The affect that that original image had on my energy and spirit was damaging. It had such a negative effect on my sense of self because it did not represent me and it essentialized me to a label and disability to be dealt with. Although, the original intent was to communicate with me where to go, from a practical perspective, it compounded my fears of being LD and associated with special education. Such benign mechanisms from institutions in the name of "helping" can have devastating effects perhaps because they do not take into account student's voice and emotionality, and hence dignity.

Figure 5. David's Canvas #4: "Healing"

The fifth canvas (Figure 6), represents the way I have begun to practice the last line on my tattoo: *How deeply did you let go?* Through a radical love anagram of safe, equity, learn, free and love for the word self-love regarding my LD and special education trauma and history to heal and transform and transcend.

Figure 6. David's Canvas #5: "Safe"

In other words, given that I feel I am stuck in letting go of a lot of my LD pain and anger, how I have come to conceptualize my healing has been through the desire to let go from a radical love approach. Love of self and others through "care, responsibility, respect, and knowledge" about my academic self (Fromm, 1956, p. 24). This is of critical importance since my

LD and special education experiences have negatively affected my mental health within educational spaces. My core-identity – self-narrativization, and personal trajectory within the big-d Discourse of special education and general education (Connor, 2005; Gee, 2001) – and who I am and becoming has become conflated with my institutional label of auditory LD from K–12 and higher educational undergraduate experiences. However, I am resilient and have always been fighting back against the assumptions embedded within the construct of LD and special education and how it has constructed them.

I know that who I am both spiritually and emotionally goes beyond the big-d Discourses, institutions and socially constructed labels from traditional special education. However, the conflation between my auditory LD label and negative experiences within special education has made me extremely upset and mad. I have come to understand these experiences as "LD trauma." It is through this freedom struggle of navigation anchored in radical love that I continue to deconstruct common-sense assumptions about dis/ability to release and let go of my "LD pain." Ultimately, I see my continuous struggle and resistance as attempting to develop the courage to radically love a system of special education that has been dehumanizing to me and reclaim my humanity. DSE has historically facilitated this process for me and, now with the conceptual and heart framework of radical love (Fromm, 1956), I hope to continue to become more fully human (Freire, 2000) through "care, responsibility, respect, and knowledge" (Fromm, 1956, p. 24).

Amy and Danielle: Challenging the Violence of Special Education by 'Working the Cracks'

As faculty teaching in special education licensure programs, we face the challenge of educating university students about the "realities" of the field of special education. We find it naïve and morally bankrupt to fail to prepare them for the institutional ableism they will encounter in today's schools. At the same time, we must propose new realities and teaching strategies to prepare our university students to challenge the violence, speak counter-narratives, and be agents of change.

Both of us have prepared teachers of students labeled with intellectual disability for a combined 20 years. Students labeled as such experience the greatest amount of segregation in schools and society (National Council on Disability, 2018) even with the language of the law (IDEA, 2004) and legal precedent indicating their right to access general education curriculum, peers, and classrooms (*Endrew F. v. Douglas County School District*, 2017; *Sacramento City School District v. Holland*, 1994; *Oberti v. Board* of *Education of the Borough of Clementon School District*, 1993). In our state of Iowa, students with intellectual disabilities are to be considered "general education students first." However, similar to states across the country, there remains great disparity between policy and reality. Our personal experiences oftentimes ground our need for exposing such disparities and the institutional ableism that produces them.

One classroom interaction experienced by Danielle exemplifies the violence of special education and the urgency of need for critical counter-strategies. About seven years ago, Danielle (as a doctoral student) accompanied several faculty who were asked to evaluate a segregated school for students with disabilities. An entire day was spent walking the halls of this county school observing, interacting with students, talking with teachers and administrators. Much was seen that could be described as troubling. However, one moment remains particularly salient due in part to the violent and visceral reaction Danielle experienced:

> Part of the "tour" of this segregated school took us to the basement of the building as teachers introduced us to a large room filled with small tables and colorful bins of various items such as mittens, marbles, rolled silverware, etc. This space was described as a work experience space... for first graders. These little humans would "clock in" with cards one would likely see on a factory floor. Then they would grab a bin and sort mittens into different colored piles. When one teacher excitedly shared that they were, "preparing them for their future," I began to have a panic attack. I knew exactly what this teacher meant – six-year-olds labeled intellectually disabled being prepared for a segregated life of subminimum wage "work" in sheltered workshops. I had to quickly leave the room as my heart was racing, throat closing in upon itself, and hives appearing on my wrists. A segregated life had already been determined for these young children under the guise of "a seamless transition."

This. This is the violence of special education. This is institutionalized ableism. This is why we must have counter-narratives grounded in DSE that can respond to such violence and offer future teachers an alternate reality. In this nontraditional essay, we examine our own autoethnographic data and offer a recent classroom exchange on behaviorism as just one example of the ways in which we critically reframe disability and prepare our students to meet, navigate, and negotiate the competing and intersecting demands of teaching. Through this section, we hope to 1) provide insight into the experiences of two DSE scholars who prepare future special education teachers – highlighting the complexities of navigating two fields that are in epistemological and ontological tension, and 2) offer one example of pushing back against the violence of traditional special education practices that lead to exclusion and segregation. We present this narrative via text message and analyze our interaction throughout using a DSE framework.

****

Danielle: *I must air grievances…*

Amy: *Go on……*

Danielle: *I've got a lot of problems with the violent and exclusionary nature of behaviorism! But as a Disability Studies in Education (DSE) scholar in a teacher preparation program I must teach them about it.*

Amy: *Uh oh.*

Danielle: *Yes! As you know, the tools of behaviorism have long served as a means to label, control, and segregate students with disabilities. The entire model is based on the idea that teachers can "modify" behavior through rewards and punishments within the overarching goal of compliance.*

****

Behaviorism is a framework and strategy deployed not only in traditional special education, but schools in general. Behaviorism, in regard to learning in general, tends to follow a "banking model" where students are viewed as empty vessels in which teachers can deposit their knowledge (Friere, 1970). Behaviorism as applied to students with disabilities, stresses the scientific modification of behavior. All behavior is conditioned by external stimuli in the form of either punishments or rewards. Therefore, in order to change the behavior, one simply needs to modify the stimulus. Kohn (1998) offers several critiques of behaviorism as the model tends to ignore student–teacher relationships, creates unequal power differentials, and in the end decreases intrinsic motivation. The need for punishment and reward inherently declines in classrooms where students can make choices about learning and tasks are of worth to explore.

Because students with disabilities may demonstrate behavior that doesn't quite fit within a teacher's definition of a "good student" (i.e., sensory/processing needs, movement, instructional pacing, wait time, etc.), they are often the recipient of greater rates of referral (Bergh & Cowell, 2013), removal from the general education classroom (Causton-Theoharis & Theoharis, 2008), denial of entry into the general education classroom (Waldron & McLeskey, 1998), and highly punitive measures such as time-out and seclusion (Diament, 2018). We must first teach our pre-service teachers to recognize these violent practices if they are to dismantle them and offer alternatives.

To once again, ground our practices in personal experience, we bring you back to Danielle's experience at the segregated school for students with disabilities. Another part of the "tour" included observations of the pre-kindergarten programs.

> First, I was taken to the "inclusive" pre-k program housed on this segregated campus. The immediate feeling upon entering this classroom space was joyous. Young children were eating snacks at little tables with friends, others were lying on brightly colored carpet squares reading books that were held by their toes, and music was playing in the corner while a teacher sang a song to one more, small group of kiddos – children with and without disabilities playing, laughing, and learning together.

> Then, I was taken to the "ABA" (or Applied Behavior Analysis) pre-k program. I was greeted with silence. All the children in this classroom were labeled with autism and were being taught 1:1 by a teaching assistant. Each child had their own table with a cardboard chorale blocking their view of any other children. No music, no books, no snack time together. A young girl who used a voice-output communication device was asked a question by the teaching assistant, "are you a boy or girl?" The child would then push the button labeled with an icon that appeared to be a girl and the device spoke, "girl." The teaching assistant would then state, "good job" and give the child an M&M. The child was asked this same question again… same response… M&M… over and over for at least five, consecutive minutes. Children with disabilities excluded, pushing buttons, complying with teacher prompts, and eating one M&M at a time. The dehumanization of it all caused those hives to slowly creep back up my wrists.

> ***

> **Amy:** Right. Behaviorism is very much reflective of a deficit understanding of students. Reeks of the medical model – meaning that disability is a deviant human difference. This highly problematic stance indicates that disability is a pathological condition innate to the student. Disabled students are in need of "fixing" and remediation. Professionals are the experts with their rational interventions (Longmore, 2003).

> ***

For readers new to DSE, it is oftentimes easiest to discuss the conceptual framing through what it is NOT. DSE is not reflective of the medical model of disability. Longmore (2003) indicates that, the medical model assumes that pathological, physiological conditions are the primary obstacle to disabled people's social integration. Defining disability as limitations in social and vocational functioning, it makes disability the exclusive and inevitable consequence of physiological impairments. It renders disability as a series of physiological, psychological, and functional pathologies… (p. 1) Instead, according to Shakespeare (2006),

> The social model demonstrates that the problems disabled people face are the result of social oppression and exclusion, not their individual deficits. This places the moral responsibility on society to remove the burdens which have been imposed, and to enable disabled people to participate. (p. 198)

***

Danielle: Yep. Time-outs, seclusion, token-economies, sticker charts, etc. These are the realities of today's classrooms, especially for disabled students. And I have to teach them about these realities if I'm ever going to expect them to change. They must be able to recognize the violence and exclusion of behaviorism in order to challenge it.

***

Both of us have seen the violent consequences of behaviorist interventions such as time-outs, seclusion, token-economies, and sticker charts: young Black and Brown boys restrained, removed and trapped in seclusion rooms; autistic children bribed with colored beads to be exchanged for a preferred activity; students who are hungry and hurting rewarded with a Superwoman sticker for staying on task. Seclusion is abuse. Period. Several school districts across our state are currently in the throes of legal battles as they try to justify their use of seclusion rooms (Jordan, 2017; Tapp, 2017). Other practices such as token-economies (where students earn small prizes for good behavior which can later be exchanged for a larger prize) and sticker charts raise ethical questions related to dependency on external rewards, depriving children of activities they desire, and the overall authoritarian nature of such "strategies" (Kohn, 1998).

***

Amy: So, we must prepare our students to "know thy enemy" so to speak. But do I feel a counter-narrative coming on as well?

Danielle: You know I love a good counter-narrative ;) Using DSE, I offer an alternative lens where disability is understood as socially constructed and the emphasis is placed on how we construct classrooms – how we create (mis)behavior – in ways that "disable" students.

Amy: Ah the social model of disability. One of my favorites. Where disability is understood within environmental, political, and social spheres. And the social model rejects the deficit model so instead, exclusion, oppression, attitudes, etc. – those are the barriers that must be remediated (Shakespeare, 2006). We must teach our students to recognize and acknowledge the violence of special education and give them the tools to enact change.

***

We identify as DSE scholars and practitioners – our understandings of disability are grounded in a social model approach where disability is framed as a complex interaction between the body, environment, place, space, discourse, policy, relationships, and intersecting identities. Disability cannot be reduced to a deficit to be "fixed" through institutions such as special education (Baglieri, Valle, Connor, & Gallagher, 2011). Impairment and the realities of the body should not be sidelined, but we also cannot ignore the environments, policies, and violence of stigma and segregation that create limitations for those labeled disabled.

Those operating within a DSE framework embrace disability as a collective yet inherently diverse minority group while promoting social justice, equitable and inclusive educational opportunities, and full and meaningful access to all aspects of society. Instead of professionals being held as the experts, DSE privileges the interests, agendas, and voices of people labeled with disability/disabled people. This privileging runs counter to traditional notions of special education, where professionals hold the power and expertise by designing and deploying student-specific interventions in the hopes of "remediating" perceived deficits. Too often such interventions result in exclusion and time away from the general education curriculum, classroom, and peers (Causton, Theoharis, Orsati, & Cosier, 2011).

***

Danielle: I agree and I try to do this. For example, I use the process of a Functional Behavior Assessment while turning it on its head – how DSE can help us (re)define words like "function" and "replacement behavior." How violent it is for children when we label them as "attention-seeking" or "avoiding." Why is it so terrible that a child wants us to pay attention to them? Or what am I doing in my classroom that is making a child want to run away? If I can show my students how an FBA can hold tremendous data to KEEP a child in a classroom instead of excluded and segregated, or how I can think about "function" as "what is my student looking for? What does s/he need?" And instead of giving a child a sticker, we need to give them love, empowerment, validation – recognize and value their competence, question how justice feels and operates in your classroom…

Amy: Ah! You are "working the cracks!"

Danielle: What do you mean, "work the cracks?"

Amy: Patricia Hill Collins (2000) uses the phrase "working the cracks" to describe how change happens. She suggests that we must use our insider perspective and membership within the system to find fissures where we can promote small change. Over time such fissures grow and result in collective change and transformation.

Danielle: Yes! I think that is what it means to do DSE work – a concsious awareness and commitment to making oneself vunerable to exclusion within uncomfortable spaces where we continue to chisel at the cracks through advocacy, resistance, and alternative praxis until our work is no longer necessary.

***

"Working the cracks" is the model we use to prepare pre-service teachers to recognize, dismantle, and re-create the rules of governance in special education. To work the cracks through DSE, we are able to breathe life into the otherwise violent and exclusionary world of special education. In the text exchange above, we demonstrated how re-framing challenging behavior is one way to "work the cracks." Other examples of this 'working the cracks' include our use of the Penny Reed (2012) approach and student-led strategies for creating Individual Educational Programs (IEP) – the IEP describes supports and services that students with disabilities are entitled to by law (IDEA, 2004).

Too often we encounter IEP meetings that are a) heavily professional/teacher-driven and b) completely written before the meeting even begins. Instead of a collaborative model that centers the voices of students and families, IEP meetings have become a place to simply report on progress and obtain signatures. Reed (2012) offers an alternative approach that is much more in the spirit of DSE and the disability rights motto of "nothing about us without us." Reed indicates that while participants in the IEP meeting may bring ideas about goals and strategies about the upcoming year, nothing should be done in writing ahead of time. The meeting is lead by a facilitator who ensures that all members are supported in a manner comfortable to them in order to voice their ideas and concerns. Using large sheets of butcher paper collaborative discussions focus on long-term goals, student strengths, short-term goals for the upcoming year, and any supports that can help the student reach her goals. And to ensure a student-centered process, the facilitator must at least check in with the student throughout to make sure their opinions are represented or can deploy several student-centered strategies ranging from a student portfolio, to an academic year soundtrack, to a snap chat session of "high" and "low" snaps from the previous year (Cowley, 2016).

DSE, thus, becomes our point of praxis where new understandings, instructional practices, and outcomes can emerge. Traditional special education holds close to the medical model insisting that students with disabilities be fixed and cured – purchase the latest reading intervention, pull the child out to a segregated setting, and provide remediated instruction. Instead, through our DSE praxis, we encourage our pre-service teachers to pay attention to the socially constructed nature of disability – pay attention to context, environment, attitudes, beliefs, relationships, and policies. Ask yourself, "Am I using books that are highly interesting? Can my student see himself represented in the book? Does he feel a sense of belonging? What instruction is he missing by being pulled from the general education classroom?"

Traditional special education also holds close to the purpose of "changing the individual through performance enhancing interventions" (Baglieri, et al., 2011, p. 268). Instead, we encourage our pre-service teachers to look toward themselves, their classrooms, and their schools for change and enhancement. Baglieri, et al. (2011) would call us "reconceptualists" (p. 267). Learning and growth are important for students – of course – but how can teachers look toward their curriculum, instruction, classroom climate, and school policies for change? Instead of preparing students with disabilities for a post-school world that may not accept them, we use DSE to problematize labels, re-center caring in education, and reduce stigma in schools. Substantial change is needed in the world of special education – we can no longer delight in an approach that excludes and stigmatizes children in such a violent way. So, we 'work the cracks' in order to create enough small fissures that can lead toward great change.

Phil: Disability, Education, and Higher Education: Academic Exclusion

I'm a White, male, full professor at a regional public university in the Midwest. I work in a department of special education, although my teaching, service, and scholarship are focused more on disability studies and mad studies, where I am generally critical of special education (and education in general) (Smith, 2010; 2014). This criticism places me at odds (to put it mildly) with almost all of the faculty members in my department. For example, a diverse group of faculty members at the university, with myself as the sole representative from the field of education, worked collaboratively a couple of years ago to develop an undergraduate minor in disability studies. As I've said elsewhere,

> [B]y disability studies, I want to mean an interdisciplinary, bricolagic exploration of ways in which disability plays out in social and cultural contexts... I understand disability as a socially constructed enterprise, and the study of it as being intentionally, explicitly, and unabashedly interdisciplinary in approach... This kind of disability studies is multiple, plural, poly – opposed to essentialism. It looks at disability through social model lenses – again, not a single way of understanding disability phenomenon. The social model of disability that I value is one placed in firm opposition to medical models, in which disability is essentialized. In medical models, people with disabilities are intentionally and explicitly Othered... Formal Othering processes of labeling and sorting, developed by Eugenicist pseudo-science and extended through special education taxonomic procedures for creating difference, meet the needs of Eurocentric, ableist, racist culture and ideology... (Smith, 2013, p. 5-6).

It is these formal Othering processes that create and extend the exclusion of disabled people from educational and civic communities in Western, Northern, Eurocentric, neoliberal, ableist, and saneist culture.

Given the inherent inter-, trans-, and cross-disciplinarity of the field and the proposed minor, we agreed (with my advocacy and full support) that it should be housed in the College of Arts and Sciences, home to the greatest number and diversity of academic fields in the university, although drawing on courses in all the other Colleges. The Dean of the College of Education, along with the Special Education Department Head, as well as other special education faculty, heard that the minor was being developed, and that it was proposed to be housed outside of Special Education. To say they were nonplussed is to put it mildly – they were damn angry. This is where contribution to this chapter starts, and where we can begin to find ways to, as Amy and Danielle put it, 'work the cracks.'

At a meeting convened by the university's Provost and Executive Vice-President, the College of Education Dean and Special Education Department Head attacked myself and other faculty members who led the disability minor development group. They insisted that it be housed in Special Education (SPED), citing that faculty in the SPED department "know about disability better than anyone else." In response, I talked briefly about the interdisciplinary nature of Disability Studies (DS), and that DS scholars typically approach their work from a social model perspective (in which disability is seen as being culturally constructed – what disables people is the institutionalized ableism of society), rather than a medical model approach (in which disability is understood as real, inherent in individual bodyminds, and is something that can be "fixed") – an approach that is typical of most special education research and practice.

I noted that DS often locates its work in the perspectives of disabled people rather than professionals, and is frequently critical of special education. I quoted disability studies scholar Simi Linton: "...special education is not a solution to the 'problem' of disability, it *is* the problem" (2006, p. 161). The Special Education Department Head denied that she was part of a medical model approach, and the College of Education Dean asserted that I was not in the mainstream of educational thinking.

The Dean and the Department Head left the meeting hurriedly. Afterwards, the Provost and the Dean for the College of Arts and Sciences stayed and talked warmly and personally about their own experiences with disability (each has disabled family members), and how that has worked out in schools. A couple of months later, a second meeting was called by the Provost's office. The Dean for the College of Education brought the Special Education Department's Curriculum and Instruction Committee co-chairs, all of whom asserted that Special Education should be the home for the proposed minor. I explained, again, about the nature of disability studies and its relationship with the field of special education; they accused me of being an enemy of the department, and openly attacked me for selling them out. I noted that my comments and work were an essential part of my scholarship, a public record of that goes back some 20 years. The Associate Provost leading the meeting said that those around the table (which included my collaborators from the College of Arts and Sciences) needed to hold space for the kind of critical scholarship and practice of which I was engaged.

Leaving the meeting, I was struck by how little those in my home department of Special Education understood the issues that I and my arts and sciences colleagues discussed; how quickly they were to engage in ad hominem attacks; how unwilling they were to see beyond the status quo; and how opposed they were to scholarship that critiqued that status quo. I reflected that faculty members and administrators outside of the College of Education seemed more understanding of the work that I engage in than were education faculty and administrators. I noted that faculty members in my home department seemed unable and unwilling to grasp issues that I talk about daily with my students. This story reflects a prime example of the kinds of exclusion that myself and others experience in the field of DS and DSE. Too often, we are relegated to the margins, seen as radical imposters who 'just don't know' about disability and SPED in ways that those holding to a medical model of disability think that they do. By excluding us, and denying the validity of our knowledge and being, traditional SPED professionals and academics deny the daily lived experience of disabled people and their families, reinforcing ableist and saneist ideologies in educational and civic communities.

This is not the first time that I've experienced this kind of personal and professional exclusion. As a practitioner in schools and communities, my critical perspective has frequently placed me at the margins of institutional, bureaucratic structures. For example, working at an agency providing community supports for people with developmental and intellectual disabilities, I was frequently confronted by case managers and support providers for my approaches advancing inclusive practices and ideas.

Still, it's frustrating and depressing to have to go outside my home department to find like-minded allies. With that said, it is also encouraging to know that there are some that I had not previously considered allies who are willing to discuss how disability relates to my work beyond SPED. In turn, within my own courses, I urge my students to challenge and change what is taken for granted in educational and civic communities. I tell them that they'll know they're doing the right work when they think they might get fired, as they say to traditional SPED professionals: "be with us or get out of the way" (Smith, 2018, p. 182). Through stories such as this one, I tell them that pushing back against ableist and saneist ideology is hard, dangerous work. But I assure them that I have their backs – that I will be an ally in the kind of essential social justice work they undertake, one that will back them up, and not back down.

Conclusive Remarks

Defining and identifying this form of educational exclusion, grounded in unacknowledged forms of ableism and violence, is of paradigmatic importance for the individual authors of this chapter and to achieve broader social transformative possibility offered by disability studies in education. Ours is a field with a critical history, from early scholars who critiqued the reliance on and limitations of the positivist paradigm to understand what is labelled as 'disability' in schools, and instead articulated holistic and constructivist alternatives to the rational-technical- and positivist-oriented methods of identification and subsequent intervention on/remediation of student disability (see, for example, the early work of scholars such as: Douglas Biklen, Burton Blatt, Ellen Brantlinger, Diane and Philip Ferguson, Lous Heshusius, Richard Iano, Tom Skrtic, and Steve Taylor). Recent contributions to scholarship in DSE have pushed notions of intersectionality, advanced the grassroots development of a neurodiversity framework, created partnerships with community scholars to utilize principles of disability justice as a tool for transformation, and uncovered spaces of disablement that are rampant across post-secondary campuses. What the emergence of DSE over the last two-plus decades has lacked, however, is a connection to broader justice-in-education dialogues, from which disability and disabled students are noticeably absent (Connor, 2012; Connor & Gabel, 2010; Gabel & Connor, 2009; Nusbaum & Steinborn, 2019; Steinborn & Nusbaum, 2019).

Our narratives of exclusion come together to require that each of us asks ourselves questions about the nature of our own educational practices and dialogue, and what are the ways that each of us might identify, understand, and make sense of the forms of exclusion of which we are complicit? How can these narratives of exclusion provide the start of doing the difficult and vulnerable work of real ally-building and solidarity towards continued action, change, and potential transformation – toward true praxis in education? Our narratives provide one such glimpse into this process of collectively and critically engaging with anti-oppressive work along lines of disability and across other markers of difference. And, additionally, how to make space for those denied participation in fruitful educational experiences, as well as fostering the chance that their voices can be appreciated for the contributions they can make toward the equity agenda in education. This is where we situate ourselves and charge the readers to ask – how can we challenge ableist logics in all forms?

References

Annamma, S. A., Ferri, B. A., & Connor, D. J. (2018). Disability Critical Race Theory: Exploring the Intersectional Lineage, Emergence, and Potential Futures of DisCrit in Education. *Review of Research in Education, 42,* 46-71.

Artiles, A. J., & Kozleski, E. B. (2007). Beyond convictions: Interrogating culture, history, and power in inclusive education. *Language Arts,* 84(4), 357.

Baglieri, S., Valle, J. W., Connor, D. J., & Gallagher, D. J. (2011). Disability studies in education: The need for a plurality of perspectives on disability. *Remedial and Special Education,* 32, 267-278.

Chang, H., Ngunjiri, F. W., Hernandez, K. C. (2012). *Collaborative autoethnography.* Walnut Creek, Calif: Left Coast Press.

Connor, D.J. (2012). Does dis/ability now sit at the table(s) of social justice and multicultural education? a descriptive survey of three recent anthologies. *Disability Studies Quarterly,* 32(3), n.p. Retrieved from http://dx.doi.org/10.18061/dsq.v32i3.1770

Connor, D. J., & Gabel, S. L. (2010). Welcoming the unwelcome: Disability as diversity. In K. Chapman & N. Hobbel (Eds.), *Social justice pedagogy across the curriculum: The practice of freedom* (pp. 201–220). New York, NY: Routledge.

Dickens, B., Reamy, M., & Nusbaum, E. A. (2015, April). Disability studies in education as a tool for transformation of the self and teaching. Paper presented at the Second City: Disability Studies in Education annual conference, Chicago, IL.

Dudley-Marling, C., & Gurn, A. (Eds.). (2010). *The myth of the normal curve.* Peter Lang.

Collins, P. H. (2000). *Black feminist thought.* New York, NY: Routledge.

Gabel, S., & Connor, D. J. (2009). Theorizing disability: Implications and applications for social justice in education. In W. Ayers, T. Quinn & D. Stovall (Eds.), *Handbook of Social Justice* (pp. 377-399). New York, NY: Lawrence Erlbaum.

Foley, D. E. (2002). Critical ethnography: The reflexive turn. *Qualitative Studies in Education, 15,* 469-490.

Freire, P. (2000). *Pedagogy of the oppressed.* New York: Bloomsbury Publishing.

Fromm, E. (1956). *The art of loving: [an enquiry into the nature of love].* Manhattan, New York City, NY: Harper.

Gallagher, D. J. (Ed.). (2004). Challenging orthodoxy in special education: Dissenting voices. Love Publishing Company.

Gee, J. P. (2001). Identity as an analytic lens for research in education. *Review of Research in Education, 25,* 99-125.

Hernández-Saca, D. I., Kahn, L. G., & Cannon, M. A. (2018). Intersectional dis/ability research: How dis/ability research in education engages intersectionality to uncover the multidimensional construction of dis/abled experiences. *Review of Research in Education, 42,* 286–311.

Hernández-Saca, D. I. (2016). *Re-Framing the master narratives of dis/ability through an emotion lens: Voices of Latina/o students with learning disabilities.* Arizona State University.

Heshusius, L. (1989). The Newtonian mechanistic paradigm, special education and contours of alternatives: An overview. *Journal of Learning Disabilities, 22,* 403 – 415.

Heshusius, L., & Ballard, K. (Eds.). (1996). *From positivism to interpretivism and beyond: Tales of transformation in educational and social research (the mind-body connection).* NY: Teachers College Press.

Humphreys, M. (2005). Getting personal: Reflexivity and autoethnographic vignettes. *Qualitative Inquiry, 11,* 840-860.

Linton, S. (2006). *My body politic: A memoir.* Ann Arbor: University of Michigan Press.

Longmore, P. K. (2003). *Why I burned my book and other essays on disability.* Philadelphia, PA: Temple University Press.

Lorde, A. (1984). *Sister outsider.* New York, NY: Ten Speed Press.

Nusbaum, E. A., & Steiborn, M. L. (2019). A "visibilizing" project: "Seeing" the ontological erasure of disability in teacher education and social studies curricula. *Journal of Curriculum Theorizing, 34*(1), 24-35.

Shakespeare, T. (2006). The social model of disability. In L. J. Davis (Ed.), *The disability studies reader* (pp. 197-204). New York, NY: Routledge.

Smith, P. (ed.) (2010). *Whatever happened to inclusion? The place of students with intellectual disabilities in education.* New York: Peter Lang.

Smith, P. (ed.) (2013). *Both sides of the table: Autoethnographies of educators learning and teaching with/in [dis]ability.* New York: Peter Lang.

Smith, P. (2018). *Writhing writing: Moving towards a mad poetics.* Fort Worth, TX: Autonomous Press.

Steinborn, M. L., & Nusbaum, E. A. (2019). Cripping human rights education with disability studies: An undergraduate reading list. *Educational Studies,* 1-16.

Ware, L. P. (2002). A moral conversation on disability: Risking the personal in educational contexts. *Hypatia, 17,* 143-172.

Ware, L. (2017). Disability Studies in K-12 Education. In L. J. Davis (Ed.). *Beginning with disability* (pp. 259-268). New York: Routledge.

Chapter 6

ANTI-BLACK RACISM, HETERONORMATIVITY, AND EXCLUSION

SHAMEKA POWELL

Ms. Espinoza and I huddled in the door of a taqueria on the city's mainly Latinx Northside on a blustery winter's Saturday morning. She had a tote bag teeming with papers slung on her left shoulder. The waitress seated us, and we slid into opposite sides of the booth. Ms. Espinoza secured her tote bag filled with student essays so it wouldn't tip over. I smiled to convey to her that I understood why she had a tote bag because I used to be a teacher, too. As our conversation picked up, she confided in me that she had chosen to leave her previous position 15 years prior at one of the city's middle schools because the students, most of whom were Black, were turning her into a racist. She said, "My experiences were so negative. A kid told me when I was pregnant, 'I'm gonna fuck you up and kill your baby.'" As our conversation continued, Ms. Espinoza shared with me that it was only after changing schools and meeting a "different type of Black student," that she was able to let go of some of her racist beliefs. As she talked, I thought to myself: Who does she think I am? Does she realize all of the horrible things she is saying to me? Does she not see me? Later that night, I stood in front of the mirror. I stared at my reflection; at my close-cropped black hair, my wood-framed black glasses, my dark brown eyes, and my Black skin, with its undertones the color of Georgia red clay. What did she see when she looked at me? Did she see who I was?

Based on my experiences as a gender non-conforming African-American educator and educational researcher, this chapter explores anti-Black racism and heteronormativity. Specifically, I present narratives that illuminate the ways I have witnessed anti-Black racism and

P.A. Boda (ed.), *Essays on Exclusion, 111–121.*

heteronormativity inform teachers' ideologies about student achievement, along with actions teachers take to help foster academic success for marginalized students. First, I narrate how teachers create the exceptional Black student trope. The trope esteems academically successful Black students as better than, and different than, their Black peers. I then argue that the trope is used to exclude, individualize success, and perpetuate anti-Black racism. Next, I offers a narrative that reveals how exclusion occurs within a classroom deemed a safe space. Specifically, I explain how heteronormative ideals about sex, gender identity, and gender expression actually marginalize those who identify as gender non-conforming.

Ultimately, this chapter is relevant to various educational stakeholders in that it suggests that exclusionary practices can occur in unexpected places – classrooms where Black students experience academic success and in classrooms deemed safe spaces. I end by offering pragmatic implications and questions that educators can use to interrogate their ideologies and practices to combat anti-Black racism and heteronormative practices that undermine marginalized students' educational opportunities.

The Exceptional Black Student Trope, Anti-Black Racism, and Exclusion

Of course, it could be argued Ms. Espinoza's comfort in telling me that Black students she taught were making her racist might have seemed as a sort of bonding experience between two educators – one a current teacher and the other, me, a former teacher. The experience might have been viewed as a time for both of us to commiserate about the stresses and challenges of teaching. After all, Ms. Espinoza had felt comfortable enough with me to divulge these struggles. Shouldn't I see that as a good thing and take it as a compliment? However, as I look back over my encounter with Ms. Espinoza, I realize that a much deeper issue was at play – anti-Black racism.

According to the Movement for Black Lives (2016), a progressive coalition of groups across North America, anti-Black racism is a "term used to specifically describe the unique discrimination, violence, and harms imposed on and impacting Black people specifically" (para. 2). As a Black person, it is taxing and demoralizing to listen to teachers recount stereotypical, deficit-themed, and downright dangerous opinions about Black people and students. I cannot recount the number of times I have heard teachers suggest that they are worried that some Black students in their classes engage in "stereotypical Black behavior" instead of doing well because they fear being picked on for "acting White". The acting-White explanation argues that Black students reject academic success for fear of being harangued as acting White by their Black peers. Although robust research debunks the specious claims that Black students exhibit oppositional culture (Lewis and Diamond, 2015; Tyson, 2011), many teachers struggle to let go of the false explanation.

As a Black educator in a field comprised overwhelmingly of White teachers, I have witnessed how teachers perpetuate anti-Black racism. For example, once I observed Ms. Phillips, a White woman, as she taught her Honors class. I noticed that although there was visible racial diversity among the students, there were few Black students. In a school where Black students were in the overwhelming majority, I was frustrated that there were so few Black students in this course. Ms. Phillips was also frustrated by the disparity in enrollment. We had had several conversations about the disparities. However, while I believed that institutional processes and teachers' pedagogical practices were implicated in creating barriers that blocked more Black students from enrolling in advanced courses, Ms. Phillips believed that Black students did not enroll in the rigorous courses because they did not value education. What's more, she perpetuated this anti-Black racist rhetoric in class! I was taken aback and offended when during my observation, she took a few moments to ask the students, "Why aren't more Black kids signing up for this class?"

I noticed that although she had posed the question to the entire class, she actually looked at the Black students as she voiced the question. Students voiced that most Black students were lazy, unmotivated, and unfocused and that was why there were so few enrolled in advanced courses throughout the entire school. Sadly, I noticed that many of the Black students nodded their heads in agreement as these anti-Black explanations were spouted. As the conversation came to an end, Ms. Phillips expressed how proud she was that a few Black students had "stepped up to the plate" and accepted the challenge of enrolling in this advanced course. Even as she characterized Black students, writ large, as lazy and unmotivated, Ms. Phillips vowed to sponsor the academic success of the few students enrolled in her class because they were "exceptional."

The narrative I share about Ms. Phillips illustrates how the exceptional Black student trope gets created and deployed within classrooms. Ms. Phillips praised Black students in her class for their tenacity and vowed to sponsor their academic needs. By sponsorship, I mean the process in which institutional agents foster, enhance, and stymie access to valued resources (Brandt, 2001). Teachers figure prominently in the narratives of Black student academic sponsorship. Take Ladson-Billings's (2005) recollections of her experiences throughout elementary school and high school, for example. A few of her teachers handpicked her from among her peers, actively involved themselves in her education in ways they did not for the majority of other students, and (periodically) followed her progress to ensure she continued to excel academically. Even more, as sponsors, teachers "...help decode institutional rules of the game, give advice, and intervene at crucial moments" (Lareau, 2015, p. 3) and they leverage their knowledge, networks, and capital to help students become upwardly mobile (Powell, 2016; Stanton-Salazar, 1997). Revealingly, this account shows how the trope gets paired with teachers' actions.

Ms. Phillips's actions might appear noteworthy and applaudable, especially when one considers that the trope of the exceptional Black student has long historical roots. During the early 20th century, this group would be described as the talented tenth. According to Du Bois (1903/1989) this elite group of Blacks would "rise and pull all [African-Americans] that are worth saving up to their vantage ground" (p. 19). These Blacks would be exceptional; they would be the men and women who would ascend the ladder of social mobility, all while lifting as they climbed. The talented tenth would save fellow Blacks from material, psychic, and cultural demise. The seductiveness of the exceptional Black student trope is that it suggests teachers should work towards such a goal. Teachers give exceptional Black students time, attention, and resources. Take the previous account, for example. Ms. Phillips vowed to sponsor and advocate for the few Black students enrolled. She wanted to make certain they excelled and outperformed Black students who did not take advanced classes.

The problem with these ideas and tropes is that they perpetuate bootstrap ideologies. Ideologies are organizing frameworks that help us make sense of social order, institutional practices, and even our experiences (Leonardo, 2003). Contextual, social, interpersonal, or systemic influences that shape opportunities and life chances are rejected when one accepts the aforementioned trope. Stated differently, what one achieves in life is the sum total of one's efforts. Even more, the trope excuses teachers from interrogating their ideologies. The narrative of the 'exceptional Black student' starts from the position that only a few Black students can and will succeed. Consequently, teachers are not encouraged to ponder how their ideologies about academic achievement and failure may be racialized.

The exceptional Black student trope is dangerous. In *Eloquent Rage: A Black Feminist Discovers Her Superpower*, Black feminist scholar Brittney Cooper (2018) explains "the trap and the burden of being exceptional is that your entire identity is wrapped up in being the only one" (p. 269).

Being one of a few in a majority White space can be overwhelming, exclusionary, and tokenizing. Black students who excel are likely to be viewed as better than and different from their Black peers. Exceptional Black students are encouraged to reject their cultural norms. They are encouraged to assimilate into Whiteness and adopt White ways of knowing and being.

Additionally, the trope is exclusionary because it perpetuates racial tokenism. Those students who are racially tokenized are expected to be Black representatives for White teachers. They are tasked with explaining complex enduring racial inequities that exist between Black students and their peers. This is what Ms. Phillips did when she posed the question about the low enrollment of Black students in advanced courses to her class. While she raised the question to the class, the way she framed the inquiry showcased a racial spotlight (Carter-Andrews, 2012) on Black students. According to Carter-Andrews (2012), racial spotlighting occurs when Black students are objectified and given unwanted attention by their White teachers and peers. In doing this, Ms. Phillips implied that Black students enrolled in advanced courses were an anomaly. Even more, her line of questioning implied that the few Black students currently enrolled in her course were interlopers. That is to say, by espousing that these Black students were exceptional, Ms. Phillips's inquiry hinted at an unspoken norm about which students should be enrolled in advanced courses. Black students were not part of that unspoken norm, even those who were exceptional. In this way, the exceptional Black student trope not only excludes those Black students who are not deemed exceptional, it actually excludes those who are deemed exceptional!

Subscribing to the exceptional Black student trope extends beyond status beliefs whereby teachers hold low expectations for Black students. Ridgeway and Erikson (2000) define status beliefs as "widely shared cultural beliefs that people who belong to one social group are more esteemed and competent than those who belong to another social group" (p. 58). Rather, the trope reveals their anti-Black racist sentiments. This is because the trope perpetuates the view that Black students and families are pathological and deficient. Pointing out how individual Black students are unlike the rest of their Black peers can only be viewed as a compliment when one believes that Black people are inherently inferior to other racial groups. Consequently, being identified as the racial exception is taken as a congratulatory.

Nigerian author Chimimanda Adichie warns that a "single story" is dangerous. The danger in the "exceptional Black student" story is that it conveys that only a few Black students are supposed to succeed. It suggests that teachers are not tasked with educating all Black students. Rather, teachers' responsibilities are to figure out which Black students are most likely to succeed and attend to their needs. This excludes other Black students. However well-intentioned, teachers who believe in the exceptional Black student trope perpetuate anti-Blackness and create barriers that exclude. If we believe from the outset that only a select few Black students can experience success, then our actions mirror that belief.

Anxiety, Heteronormativity, and Exclusion

The narratives we tell ourselves dictate the actions we take toward inclusion and educational equity. While schools are framed as inclusive and welcoming spaces that value everyone, the experiences of sexual and gender minorities contradict those false narratives. I am a Black queer person, one who was assigned female at birth and is gender non-conforming. I present as masculine of center (Cole, 2010). The term masculine of center was coined by B. Cole (2010) and it used to

> recogniz[e] the cultural breadth and depth of identity for lesbian/queer womyn and gender nonconforming/trans people who tilt toward the masculine side of the gender spectrum – including a wide range of identities such as butch, stud, aggressive/AG, macha, dom, trans masculine, boi, etc. (n.p.)

Given my identities, I am intimately aware of how unwelcoming and unsafe schools can be for those who transgress heteronormative norms. Take an encounter I had in a classroom deemed as a "safe space," for example, that I unpack for the reader below.

I was seated in the back of Ms. Stein's room and was out of anyone's direct line of sight. "Remember," Ms. Stein told her eleventh-grade literature and rhetoric students, "sex, gender, and sexuality are not the same. Now, let's continue the conversation." On the board behind her, Ms. Stein had written three Essential Questions:

- What is the purpose of gender? What is its role, function, significance?
- What are the strengths and weaknesses of participating and performing gender?
- Would you change/reconsider your relationship to gender? Would you make any changes for society as a whole?

My stomach was in knots. My hands were clammy. Sweat pooled around my neck. The collar of my shirt was drenched. I loosened my tie and cleared my throat in an attempt to calm myself. Would my anxiety show, I wondered? My discomfort radiated off me in waves. I was worried that my face would reveal what I felt. I hoped no one noticed; not Ms. Stein and not any of these students. But I knew. I knew my body was being read. How could my body not be read? I was the only visibly gender non-conforming person present and, especially in contexts such as this, my identity was certainly more visible than ever.

As I sat in the back of the room panicking, Ms. Stein recounted a story about the time Sam, her son, put on her heels:

> Several years ago, when Sam was 3, he put on my heels and my husband was about to freak out! I could see it on his face but before he could say anything, I stopped him, and I asked him, "What was wrong with our son wearing Mama's heels?" she recollected. "What do you think he said?" She made a sweeping gesture with her hands as she opened the discussion.

Students argued that it was Ms. Stein's husband who was wrong for trying to stop their son from trying on her shoes. "Kids just like to dress up," one student offered. Several others voiced their agreement. One Black boy mentioned that when he was younger, he had been really sensitive and had cried a lot. He explained that people dear to him would often respond with, "Boys don't cry! Toughen up!" He explained that as a consequence, he did not cry much anymore. Others chimed in with ways they had experienced gendered socialization and expectations. I listened as the conversation continued.

I began to relax my body and loosen my clenched teeth. Maybe I was being paranoid, I thought to myself. They had not conflated gender and sexuality. Students were doing a great job of interrogating gender norms and expectations. A few girls even pointed out how the school's dress policy was only enforced for female students but not male students. A Latina student suggested that the policy was unevenly enforced because the school, like society, policed female sexuality. Within a second, a male student broke in and stridently declared, "I don't agree with homosexuality. Same-sex attraction is not natural. I respect homosexuals, but I don't accept their lifestyles." There was a quiet murmur of agreement from a few students and I saw several students surreptitiously glance my way. Displeasure, anxiety, and frustration all flashed across my face before I was able to return to a blank look.

Ms. Stein quickly interrupted and reminded everyone that "this is a safe space for everyone" and that "everyone is welcome here." Several students shook their heads in agreement, and a few snapped their fingers. All I could think about, however, was that this class was not a safe space, not for gender non-conforming people like me, along with anyone who transgressed heterosexist assumptions. Heterosexism is "bias or discrimination in favor of 'opposite-sex' relationships and sexual attractions and in favor of heterosexual-identified people" (Barker and Scheele, 2016, p. 244). Relatedly, heteronormativity is the belief that all people are heterosexual, and that heterosexuality is the default and rightful norm.

Granted, discussions about sex, gender identity, and gender expression can be difficult to have if for no other reason than the frequency with which the terms are incorrectly used interchangeably. The concepts are not synonymous, either. For instance, biological sex is a term used to refer to one's anatomy. Biological sex is most often classified at birth as female, male, or intersex. However, gender identity captures how one feels internally about their gender. Woman, man, genderqueer, and trans are just a few of the labels used to denote one's gender identity. Equally important, how one outwardly presents themselves is their gender expression. The categories of masculine and feminine are most often used to capture one's external display of gender. It goes without saying that gender is socially constructed and is shaped by cultural norms, expectations, and behaviors. When one's gender identity and gender expression align with societal expectations about one's biological sex, then one is said to be cisgender.

It is important to recognize that binaries such as male/female, man/woman, masculine/feminine are exclusionary and limiting. These categories do not provide space for those who do not fit into or who transcend these dichotomies. There are many people, students among them, who identify as gender non-conforming, gender non-binary, and more. Those who identify as gender non-conforming do not dress, behave, or otherwise comport themselves in a way that aligns with societal expectations of that sex. Those who identify as gender non-binary may not identify with the man/woman binary at all. Because we have expectations of how boys and girls, men and women, are supposed to act, we often marginalize those people who express their gender differently. Take the common expression, "boys don't cry," for example. Embedded within that statement is the belief that masculinity, and by extension boys and men, are supposed to be tough and unemotional. Conversely, girls and women are expected to be soft and emotional.

My story of being made to feel like an outsider in a nominally inclusive space testifies to the exclusionary force of heterosexism and heteronormativity. One's gender presentation does not reveal one's sexuality. The distinction between gender identity and sexual orientation has been described with the pithy explanation: gender identity is who you go to bed as while sexual orientation is who you go to bed with. It remains the case, however, that gender non-conforming educators and students often navigate school contexts that are hostile, heterosexist and heteronormative. Well-known Twitter personality, Robert Jones, Jr, who tweets under the handle @SonofBaldwin writes, "We can disagree and still love each other, unless your disagreement is rooted in my oppression and denial of my humanity and right to exist."

Pragmatic Implications

In order to combat anti-Black racism, teachers must interrogate their beliefs about Black students, achievement, and failure. They may also ask themselves the following questions:

- Do I believe all Black students can be successful?
- If I believe all Black students can be successful, how many have been successful in my classes? Why? Why not?
- What are some characteristics and behaviors I think successful Black students exhibit?
- Which students do I praise? Which students do I punish? Why?
- What kind of messages do I send to all students about Black student success and failure?

Certainly, asking these questions might cause discomfort and feelings of unease. Consider this, for instance: if you believe that all Black students can be successful but that their success is contingent upon behaving in certain ways – ways that demand compliance and subservience – then there is the likelihood that you have privileged, dominant racial expectations of behavior. As a result of that, you may have failed to foster success for Black students who did not comport themselves in these racially dominant ways. Surely, these revelations about one's self are never easy to admit and are even harder to come to terms with. I imagine many people would not want to know that they did such things. However, it is only by engaging in critical self-reflective practices that teachers can even begin to disrupt taken-for-granted assumptions and practices they engage in that exclude students.

Additionally, administrators and teachers must do more than simply pay lip service to inclusivity. Where issues of gender identity and expression are concerned, teachers must constantly interrogate their own assumptions about gender norms and provide opportunities for students to do the same. Equally important, administrators and teachers must stop framing the phrase "inclusive spaces" as a noun. Rather, they must change their thinking and recognize the phrase as an ongoing action-oriented process. That is to say, spaces are constantly in the process of being made inclusive and safe, they never 'become' but, rather 'are becoming.'

In the recently released and widely acclaimed book, *When They Call You a Terrorist: A Black Lives Matter Memoir*, Black Lives Matters activists and community organizers Patrisse Khan-Cullors and asha bandele (2018) explain that even in spaces marked by commitments to fighting oppression, the voices of the most vulnerable and most marginalized sometimes get silenced. For example, Black transwomen are uniquely marginalized by intersecting oppressive systems. Yet, Khan-Cullors recounts that even as she and other freedom fighters journeyed to Ferguson, Missouri to protest police officer Darren Wilson's extrajudicial killing of Michael Brown, a Black teenager, the activists failed to amplify the voices of Black transwomen and "did little to ensure their visibility" (p. 293). She goes on to share that it is only by "being self-reflective about and dismantling cisgender privilege and uplifting Black Trans folk, especially Black Transwomen" (p. 276) that freedom fighters can begin to rectify their (unintentionally) exclusionary practices.

I share this account to draw a parallel as to what must occur within schools across the nation. In summary, we must realize that schools are sites of exclusion. Even more important, administrators and teachers must realize that it is those students who are disproportionately impacted by intersecting oppressive institutional policies and practices that get to decide whether a space is safe and inclusive. Only then, can exclusion begun to be addressed and dismantled.

REFERENCES

Barker, M. J. & Scheele, J. (2016). *Queer: A graphic history*. London: Icon Books.

Brandt, D. (2001). *Literacy in American lives*. Cambridge University Press: New York.

Carter-Andrews, D. (2012). Black achievers' experiences with racial spotlighting and ignoring in a predominantly White high school. *Teachers College Record*, 114, 1–46.

Cooper, B. (2018). *Eloquent rage: A Black feminist discovers her superpower*. New York: St. Martin's Press.

Cole, B. (2010). "Brown boi project: About us". Retrieved from www.brownboiproject.org/about-us.

Du Bois, W.E.B. (1903/1989). *The souls of Black folk*. New York: Bantam.

Jones, R. Jr. [@SonofBaldwin]. (2015, August 18). "We can disagree and still love each other unless your disagreement is rooted in my oppression and denial of my humanity and right to exist." [Tweet]. Retrieved from https://twitter.com/SonofBaldwin/status/633644373423562753.

Khan-Cullors, P., & Bandele, A. (2018). *When they call you a terrorist: A Black Lives Matter memoir*. New York, NY: St. Martin's Press.

Ladson-Billings, G. (2005). *Beyond the Big House: African American educators on teacher education*. New York, NY: Teachers College Press.

Lareau, A. (2015). Cultural knowledge and social inequality. *American Sociological Review, 80*(1), 1-27.

Leonardo, Z. (2003). Discourse and critique: Outlines of a post-structural theory of ideology. *Journal of Education Policy, 18*, 203-214.

Lewis, A. E., & Diamond, J. B. (2015). *Despite the best intentions: How racial inequality thrives in good schools*. New York, NY: Oxford University Press.

Movement for Black Lives. (2016). "A vision for Black lives: Policy demands for Black power, freedom, and justice". Retrieved from policy.m4bl.org.

Powell, S. N. (2016). Sifting for success: A multi-sited ethnographic account of teachers fostering academic success for (some) Black students. In R. Hopson (Ed.), *New directions in educational ethnography*. UK: Emerald Group Publishing.

Ridgeway, C. L., & Erickson, K. G. (2000). Creating and spreading status beliefs. *American Journal of Sociology, 106*, 579-615.

Stanton-Salazar, R. (1997). A social capital framework for understanding the socialization of racial minority children and youths. *Harvard Educational Review, 67*(1), 1-41.

Tyson, K. (2011). *Integration interrupted: Tracking, Black students, and acting White after Brown*. New York, NY: Oxford University Press.

Chapter 7

THE OUTSIDER WITHIN

Thoughts and Musings on Exclusion as Stranger-Making

DEBBIE SONU

The Intent

I am drawn to the everyday encounters that make one feel strange, those intersubjective encounters that are felt on the skin, those words and gestures that figure one as out of place, as not belonging. Never outside relations of power and traces of colonial histories, the possibilities of our social interactions, including how we determine the parameters of inclusion and exclusion, occur at the site of our encounters with others. When we come into contact, we differentiate familiarity from strangeness. We establish the criteria upon which to recognize our communities, how to distinguish ourselves from them and from theirs. It is through the act of stranger-making that the salience of distributed precarity, e.g. race, ethnicity, gender, class, affects the freedom to move through certain spaces, to attain certain privileges and occupy certain lands.

Institutional policies, including those in schools and universities, respond to such exclusionary patterns by enacting their neoliberal interpretations for diversity and multiculturalism. Most organizations these days have a report somewhere that outlines in bulleted form the policies and practices designed to ensure the presence of belonging spaces. They track their demographics and seek to equalize underrepresentation accordingly. There are officers, attorneys, workshops and training sessions, all dedicated to ensure that those most often excluded are marginalized no

P.A. Boda (ed.), *Essays on Exclusion*, 123–133.

more. An apparatus indeed, great tension often arises between the efficiency model of management, the revolutionary aims of the people, the more careful and studied approach of the theoretician, and the benevolent bystander who nods in camaraderie but continues work as usual. Members from all these parties have been guilty, at one time or another, of fixing subjective experience into quantifiable categories of inclusion, dangerously replacing conversations on history and power with an oversimplification of identity and the mere adding of diverse bodies into the normative mix.

The intent of this chapter is to think about the theme of exclusion in several ways:

- as it materializes through contact: how bodies read each other
- as the formation of communities: how shared qualities also exclude
- as traces of history: how the past always matters
- as an institutional concern: how even inclusion can discriminate.

Littered throughout are various stories, familiar yet distinct. They are enfleshed by the tensions that one experiences when not being able to pass in the world, the sudden jolt of the slur, the lingering afterthought, the way we carry these stabbings and jabs into our homes and schools, and out into the playgrounds and sidewalks, how they turn us away from each other and perhaps even more critically, how they turn us away from ourselves. The stories are many, and while incidents of exclusion are often marred in pain, what must be remembered, too, is the potential for such events to stir up an openness, a possibility, an unsettling of old habits, stereotypes, and prejudices.

Exclusion Is Stranger-Making

In her book, *On Being Included: Racism and Diversity in Institutional Life*, Sara Ahmed (2012) writes that the act of stranger-making is not that the stranger is unknown, but that it is constructed as unfamiliar and distanced. The stranger, then, is a figure that has already been recognized; it is somebody affectively judged as having a particular set of qualities that warrants them stopped at the border, inadmissible, turned away. As often an object that, at the same time, "captivates us, beckons and rejects" (Kristeva, 1991, p. 3), we recognize the stranger, not because we lack knowledge about them, but because we have already read their bodies. We have differentiated them as strange and kept them in their place. Thus, the stranger is not a thing, but rather an address towards someone we have yet to encounter.

This description helps us to destabilize the stranger as a fixed object and instead demonstrates how we make strangeness happen. From our very first moment of contact, we are moved by, with, and into this other being. We pull them into our evolving beliefs about what belongs in our proximity. This exhibition of what we prefer to be near and what we keep distanced includes not only the bodies, but the space, the history, the sociopolitical context, unconscious desires, the internalization of discrimination, the lessons learned from childhood, from family, community, and the national imaginary. Both personal and historical, even the slightest of exchanges are greatly encoded and complex. They can be both fleeting and forgotten, corrosive and overwhelming.

> You sit next to the man on the train, bus, in the place, waiting room, anywhere he could be forsaken. You put your body there in proximity to, adjacent to, alongside, within. (Rankine, 2014, p. 131)

In her poem "Making Room", Claudia Rankine throws us into the psychic volley that occurs when the gestures of others in everyday encounters signify a perception of the strange. The woman standing in the train puts into motion a sudden rush of negotiations for the seated man. The seat beside him is unoccupied. She spots the seat, glances over at the man, and prefers to stand. Perhaps she never intended to sit, perhaps something strange made her recoil. Operating through a politics of perception, the stranger is felt in the body of the one who makes such an address. If the stranger gets too close, we might pull away, or avert our eyes; in some cases, the stranger can induce one to attack, defend, ridicule, pity or stare. It is also felt in the stranger – he combs through a list of reasons, draws assumptions, takes it personally, and leaves with impressions.

The difference between the body and the body politic is the recognition that beings cannot be fully defined by their labels, but are placed into categories of comparison that make visible and invisible how they come to be seen. Nothing here is natural and every incident is an example of how, as said by Judith Butler (1997), our visible identities – the tone of flesh, the shape of eyes, the texture of hair – become the interlocutors that elicit different addressivities. Oftentimes, the address is to remove those who impose a threat to the norm of one human, one kind, or one quality of being. Other responses are not to expel, but to maintain the strange within existing structures and internally fraught institutions that depend upon their very service as laborers, or scapegoats, or models of immorality, or as Christina Sharpe (2014) describes, plantation geographies, operationalized through "continuous surveillance by camera and police helicopter, stop-and-frisk, curfews, the restrictions imposed on people without papers, minimal to no employment opportunities, probation officers, the judicial system, police pressures on family members, etc." More progressive circles can fetishize the other (Cheng, 2001). They can long and desire their contact, devour its culture (hooks, 1992), and commodify its difference as a source of pleasure or enchantment.

Exclusion and Community-Building

"One time," shares Alice, a student in my class, "some kids just decided to come up to me and pulled their eyes apart to make them squintier. They started singing, 'Me Chinese, me Chinese', and after that, I realized they were making fun of my eyes. I went home that day and cried. I specifically remember asking my parents if there was something wrong with me. It made me feel bad about my body, and it made me feel worse that there was nothing I could do to change it." At the sweet age of seven, Alice moves into an all-White elementary school in Maryland and for the first time, learns she is Chinese. The places and cultures she will have to negotiate in this new geographic landscape are many, but here she is suddenly denied her belonging and thrown into a whirlwind of confusion.

At first, she is unsure of what it all means, and her body explodes into tears. She had always moved seamlessly in and out of social spaces in Guangzhou, but here, as a child of the United States, her body becomes a figure of difference that is not merely found or characteristic of Alice, but rather, established as a relation among bodies who are defining the terms of her normalcy. What is exercised are the recurring tropes and predictable plotlines of the racial slur. The pulling back of the eyes publicly governs who is to be encountered as familiar and who is to be excluded and made strange. In the enforcement of "we," she has been seen, heard, and felt as "the uncommon," a force of exclusion that puts into motion both a history of anti-Asian sentiment and the internalization of self as the object of derision.

In a way similar to identity, we typically think of community or belonging as cohesion, sameness, or commonality. Yet, we can also think of community as a consequence of our impulse to differentiate and expel that which does not fit. A community, then, is the coming together of bodies, who under the register of familiarity or likeness, have read others and produced them as strange, foreign, or even threatening and dangerous to that on the inside. Under the imaginary coherence of "we," this inter-embodiment (Ahmed, 2000) always operates on the premise of difference.

These encounters with difference involve certain cultural rules and procedures for how we deal with the other and how their bodies come to be read and felt. Such as in the case of Alice, as bodies are invited into or expelled from a community, the social spaces they inhabit are discursively expanded or diminished. Therefore, the bodies within an inclusive community are not necessarily bonded under some common denominator, but rather these bodies, each with their own particularities and differences, have somehow found attraction to each other and have come to establish the parameters of what is recognized as assimilable.

The body, then, is both a focal point of connection and a reason for separation. It is upon the visible exterior of Alice that the cultural rules of inclusion and exclusion are drawn by her classmates. This does not mean that we should aim for the erasure of her difference, nor should she be included through her assimilation into some sort of communal and consensual "we." Both of these approaches would corrode the ability to understand what identity actually reveals about the human condition, not as rationale endeavor but as affectively built through quotidian struggles both elusive and overtly felt in time and in place (Alcoff, 2006). As Ahmed and Jackie Stacey (2001) offer, what is this "fleshy interface between bodies and worlds" (p. 1)? Alice's body becomes an allure that seduces her White classmates into her proximity and although they engage her through the simultaneity of their abjection and ridicule, this act of exclusion has brought them together in a precarious and vulnerable encounter.

Claudia Rankine and Alice tell stories of how the power of affect can govern the attributions of exclusion. Affect, if we follow Michalinos Zembylas (2006), differs from emotion in that it is not just a feeling, but rather a force that shapes the capacity of the body to act. It comes into play at the site of encounters with others and sets the terms upon which we experience our outside world. It is that shadowy sense, that feeling of, that something-out-there, the sublime. As Alice and her White classmates come close, she is affected by their gesture, a border has become erected and the space has been marked by the limits of its inclusion. Stranger-making, then, is not just a rational interaction between two individuals, but involves an ungraspable, but knowable, a movement that unfolds as beings come together within sociopolitical contexts. Stranger-making is space-making in that it brings together worlds and sets the limits of their welcome. After all, says Dorian Massey (2005), space is but an embodiment of social networks.

Exclusion In Nation Culture

According to Jodi Melamed (2006), the very idea of a racially inclusive national culture was animated during wartime to promote manifest destiny and American exceptionalism, while serving to mask the internal policies and procedures that naturalized racial privilege, discrimination, and violence. In this aporetic landscape, the 'foreigner within' (the person of color, the poor, the woman, the disabled, the transient, uneducated, androgynous) is tossed around by the double bind of acceptance and rejection, of being strange and welcome. All the while the U.S. is seen as the gallant savior, propped by a marginality that has always been central to the making of the mainstream.

"The next day," continues Alice, "one of the kids decided to yell out, in front of the whole class, really loudly, 'Alice is a chink,' and then everyone in the class started to laugh. I remember trying to figure out the meaning of the word and when I did, I was very hurt. I was shocked that they had a word for it."

The demarcation of difference, in both the making of the stranger and determining who belongs, establishes a national imaginary that incorporates the other as the "we" of the nation, at the same time that it demonstrates that it is "we" who has to live with "them." Exclusion, then, is also about what happens when social collectivities are disturbed, when a foreign object enters into the membership of a particular group, or when a member of the group is suddenly determined to be strange and unwanted. For those living in our racial imaginary, it is not assimilation that prevents one from being real, but the haunting experience of not being secure within such a fiction, the fiction and fantasy of citizenship, of liberty, of social mobility and attainment, all of which comes into contradiction at the site of inclusion and rejection.

While language has the power to assert the silenced into a field of recognition, it also carries the power to injure, to make vulnerable, to bring the subject into a discourse of precarity (Butler, 1997; 2003). This means that the act of 'naming' is actually a discursive practice that produces the subject rather than simply reflects or describes it. The stamping of 'chink,' a term traced back to late-19th-century British labor exploitation and racism, spins Alice into a place of unanticipated disorientation. Yet, perhaps this is what Toni Morrison (2017) confers, when she says the stranger shines its most revealing light, not on those deemed strange, but on those who work to establish institutions, policies, and practices to ensure one's strangeness.

In *The Melancholy of Race*, Anne Anlin Cheng (2001) points to Freud's development of melancholia to suggest that racism is hardly ever a clear rejection, but rather, a holding of the other in a psychical relationship close enough to be constituted by its difference. Melancholia is particularly acute in the United States because it proclaims its founding ideals as freedom, liberty, and equality, but then time and time again, disavows or covers over its many betrayals (Cheng, 2001).

Long before the period known as the Yellow Peril reached its height during the Second World War (WWII), a network of anti-Chinese groups (many of which would reemerge as anti-Japanese) passed laws that limited Asians access to the rights protected under citizenship. The Naturalization Act of 1870 prohibited them from voting, serving on juries, prevented them from testifying against Whites in court, and designated Asians as permanent "aliens" who were ineligible to own land or real estate, all of which prevented Asians from participating in the country's legal, political, and financial systems. Racial tension and violence erupted at the proximity of Chinese bodies. Although they were recruited into the mining and railroad industries in the mid-19th century, they were simultaneously seen as threats to the racial purity of those who belonged on the inside. Their ability to migrate across transnational borders was halted by policies such as the Chinese Exclusion Act of 1882, which became the reason for labor recruiters to target Japanese workers, which then triggered anti-Japanese sentiment long before the bombing of Pearl Harbor.

Fifty years later, during WWII, Franklin Roosevelt signs Executive Order 9066 and begins to establish Japanese internment camps with the intent of preventing espionage on American shores. Military zones are established in California, Washington, and Oregon, the states with the largest Japanese American populations. These camps, located on indigenous lands despite protest from tribal council, affected the lives of 117,000 people, the majority of whom were American citizens. As part of an agreement among foreign ministers from Argentina, Brazil, Chile, Mexico, the United States, Uruguay, and Venezuela, other countries began to follow. Canada relocated 21,000 of its Japanese residents, Mexico enacted its own version and almost 2,264 Latin Americans of Japanese descent from Peru, Brazil, Chile and Argentina, were sent to the United States for containment. In 2007, the U.S. Senate Committee on Homeland Security and Government Affairs created a commission to investigate the facts and circumstances around Japanese who were on a "blacklist" at the American embassy in Peru and were kidnapped and deported at gunpoint by the Peruvian police and sent to internment camps in Texas and New Mexico.

In these historical periods, the Chinese and Japanese culture has been politically conceived as something an individual has or possesses and is immediately associated with heritage, or a fixed notion of origin. This 'stranger culture,' one that evokes foreignness, exoticism, ridicule, mystery and enchantment, is produced as an object free of contradiction and complexity. Cultural differences within categories of Asianness are contained and given shape by government and economic policies, which is seen at the ease in which the rights of U.S. citizens can be suddenly revoked, as if the promises of multiculturalism rested on the kinds of services and permissions allowed by those who administer its government.

Inclusion While Exclusion

Yet for spaces of inclusion to mean something other than the redomestication and resubordination of other such differences, it will have to develop a sense of cohesion through a new form of engagement that does not re-territorialize the existing relations of power. Seemingly benevolent promises of inclusion, particularly those operationalized through the neoliberal discourse of diversity, representation, and multiculturalism, often fail to include reference to the ways in which divisions of power continue to render educational institutions as exclusive places. Said differently, policies are not sufficient to make a space inclusive. It matters what is done in that space.

The simultaneity of inclusion and exclusion is clear in this account from my friend and colleague, Jolene as she writes:

> While it might seem that being a Black professor at a HBCU would be more comfortable and the environment more nurturing than at a predominantly White institution, for women and queer faculty just the opposite is often the case. HBCUs were first established to provide African Americans with the opportunity to receive a quality education after the Civil War when Blacks could not attend segregated White colleges in the South. Long-held homophobia in both the Black Church and Black communities contribute to an uncomfortable atmosphere at HBCUs for LGBTQ people. As within the Black church, there is a 'pervasive 'don't ask, don't tell' reflex'. There is of course nothing overtly stated, however for any remotely self-aware queer student or faculty, widespread heterosexism and homophobia dissuades many from 'coming out.'

She continues:

Being bi-sexual it was safer to talk about men I found attractive, than my girlfriend at home. I waited until I knew a colleague very well, and their attitudes about the LGBTQ community, before revealing that part of my identity. As a result, there was only a handful that I could be genuinely authentic with, preferring to have that part of me be invisible rather than deal with the possible or actual repercussions. I did not want to be subject to the heterosexist values of the institution.

For Jolene and others, to talk about LGBTQ issues is to occupy a space of saturated tension. It is because their sense of constriction that estranged individuals decide not to pose the problem aloud. Instead, we see her receding from those she perceives to not understand, opening herself only to those with whom she assumes a shared experience. Jolene's double strategy of attachment and detachment signals that the resolution to a history of racial discrimination is not easily resolved in the making of new communities and organizations, but that relationships of togetherness are always symptomatic of their intersectionalities.

Therefore, communities are not based on characteristics of sameness, but are created through the perception that this person may understand. Although Jolene's inclusion into this institutional space may be predicated on a perception of racial consonance, it continues to ask for her recommitment to the terms of this inclusion. If the politics of belonging (Yuval-Davis, 2011) comprise specific political projects aimed at constructing particular collectivities, then the politics of exclusion includes both the affective force of non-conformity and inferiorization, and the social, economic, and political effects of many such differentiations. This can occur, as we see with Jolene, even in the most inclusive of spaces.

Collectives, then, are built upon the very work that we need to do to get closer to each other, without simply appropriating the other as evidence of policy, or in service to our own objectives. At the same time, we can also see how emotions of self-denial and refusal are not just psychological states, but cultural practices. Under what conditions does Jolene refuse to be a subject within the heteronormativity of her university? How does her sense of things have affective power and dictate her movement through the social and material world? She turns inward, secretive and silent. She begins to align herself to the popular ideology of what is considered familiar and strange and even within a space of proclaimed belonging, she has given up on the terms of inclusion, and foreclosed herself to the possibility of her intervention in the world. Her bodily response, drawn from the sediment of history and a sense of it-just-doesn't-feel-right, is usually responded to by a cajoling of testimony and narrative. As if speaking her silence will overturn the structures that make her strange.

Concluding Thoughts

There are many examples of exclusion within inclusion and they demonstrate that the formation of unity, or more often solidarity, cannot be resolved through an obliteration of difference, and certainly not through the presumption that one has been sufficiently recognized by the other. Rather, only through a vigilant remaking of relationships such that additional forms of subordination do not become reinstituted as the condition of its own possibility can the subject be liberated from the cycle of inclusionary spaces that exclude. For us educators, this means that we cannot rely on identity as the sole explanation of difference and more importantly, that we must be cautious when our curriculum speaks of consensus and community as sameness.

It may not be enough to form communities through the definition and categories of not being included. But, rather, what is needed is attention to what is becoming altered in that space, the constantly reformulation and decentering of that which perpetually comes to be seen as familiar in relation to the strange, and to open up blockages and restrictions for movement within and across spaces. One such way is to refuse the commodity object, the turning of culture into an object that is then valued and desired for its difference. This process detaches the stranger from the social relationships that have deemed it strange and produces tropes and fads that render culture a material thing to be consumed. It conceals how the stranger comes into being through the marking out of inhabitable spaces, but also as bell hooks (1992) writes, how the strange comes to be used instrumentally in service to those who desire to be viewed as progressive and culturally aware. The inclusion of those underrepresented and excluded in the institution must be accompanied with a constant vigilance to power and history so as not to reterritorialize such spaces with the subordination of new forms of discrimination. For this, we need a conceptualization of difference that includes affective understandings of our lives in the midst of others, to continue the struggle at the site of encounters with a multitude of differences, and to create spaces that honor diversity in ways that sustain the realities and meanings of difference itself.

REFERENCES

Alcoff, L. M. (2006). *Visible identities: Race, gender, and the self.* New York: Oxford University Press.

Ahmed, S. (2000). *Strange encounters: Embodied others in post-coloniality.* New York: Routledge.

Ahmed, S. (2012). *On being included: Racism and diversity in institutional life.* Durham, NC: Duke University Press.

Ahmed, S., & Stacey, J. (Eds.). (2001). *Thinking through the skin.* London: Routledge.

Butler, J. (1997). *The psychic life of power: Theories in subjection.* Palo Alto, CA: Stanford University Press.

Butler, J. (2003). The question of social transformation. In E. Beck-Gernsheim, J. Butler, & L. Puigvert (Eds.), *Women & Social Transformation* (pp. 1–28). New York: Peter Lang.

Cheng, A. A. (2001). *The melancholy of race: Assimilation and hidden grief.* New York: Oxford University Press.

hooks, b. (1992). *Black looks: Race and representation.* New York: Routledge.

Kristeva, J. (1991). *Strangers to ourselves.* New York: Columbia University Press.

Massey, D. (1994). *Space, place and gender.* Minneapolis, MN: University of Minneapolis Press.

Melamed, J. (2006). The spirit of neoliberalism: From racial liberalism to neoliberal multicultural. *Social Text, 24*(4), 1–24.

Morrison, T. (2017). *The origin of others.* Cambridge, MA: Harvard University Press.

Rankine, C. (2014). Citizen. Minneapolis, MN: Greywolf Press.

Sharpe, C. (2014, August 8). Black life, annotated. *The New Inquiry.* Retrieved from https://thenewinquiry.com/black-life-annotated/

Yuval-Davis, N. (2011). *The politics of belonging: Intersectional contestations.* London: SAGE Publications.

Zembylas, M. (2006). Emotional ecology: The intersection of emotional knowledge and pedagogical content knowledge in teaching. *Teaching and Teacher Education, 23,* 355–367.

Chapter 8

HISTORICAL EXCLUSION AS AN ONUS FOR INCLUSION AND HOME IN STEM

REANNA S. ROBY, ANGELA CALABRESE BARTON, LOUISE, ARI, SHAREE & CHLOE

Introduction

Louise skipped out from the center of the circle of chairs towards the red couch with her arms open wide and proclaimed loudly, "This is how I feel included!" As she plunked down on the couch, she elaborated, "This couch and rainbow carpet makes me feel included. It's like how comfortable the couch is, the carpet and the room. It's like, Wooo Woooo Wooo! I want to be included in everything!" Louise stands up again, and circles around, pointing in all directions around the room.

Louise's proclamations came when she and I (Angie) were discussing what it meant to feel included and excluded in STEM (science, technology, engineering and mathematics). She had arrived early at her after-school STEM club, located in a vibrant community center, and has asked me if she could help set up. We started by moving chairs into a circle for an opening discussion. As we set the chairs, I was telling her about the plan for the afternoon. I had said to her that I wanted to start our session with a conversation with the other youth on inclusion/exclusion. I wished to better build into our program practices that the youth felt promoted greater inclusion. As I told her about this goal, I had asked her for help in how we might best have this conversation. It was then that she skipped out from the center of the chairs and over to the couch.

P.A. Boda (ed.), Essays on Exclusion, 135–147.

The couch and the carpet that Louise referenced were added to the STEM room 18 months prior and about one year before Louise joined. The youth in the club had lobbied for a couch and rainbow carpet because as one of the youth, Rayna, put it, young people needed a place to "let off steam," "be frustrated," "be themselves," and "think." They wanted a place where they could "have snacks," "play," "listen to music," and "just hang out." The youth here not only speak of the frustrations of learning STEM, but also negotiating/navigating STEM towards transforming it and the role it can play in their lives. As Kairee noted, her STEM-rich work of designing and prototyping a portable seat-heater for the public bus was like "going to hell and back" as they work to re-create STEM in ways that matter to them and their communities.

For Louise and for her peers before her, like Rayna and Kairee, the couch was about much more than having a comfortable place to sit, although this is important, given their long days in hard school chairs. It was about re-making their STEM room into a place that is welcoming of their full and complex lives. It is about making space, physically, spiritually and socially in STEM, where space was not always made available to them. Louise's comments about the couch speak directly to experiences of inclusion and exclusion.

In this chapter, we explore experiences of inclusion/exclusion in STEM with a group of middle-school African-American girls who participated in and helped to co-construct their after-school STEM-rich maker club. We take a Critical Race lens to this work, calling particular attention to bell hooks's conceptualizations of homeplace as a way to understand the anti-racist practices of inclusionary homeplace-making practices by these young women, and their efforts to redefine inclusion and exclusion.

The Harsh Worlds of STEM and Making

Traditionally, STEM education has valued and reflected masculine Eurocentricity in practice (Mensah & Jackson, 2018). As a means of critiquing both STEM and making, we employ Critical Race Theory as a conceptual lens and methodology. Based in the practices and traditions of jurisprudence, Critical Race Theory (CRT) is an outgrowth of Critical Legal Studies (CLS) (Crenshaw, Gotanda, Peller & Thomas, 1995). CRT as a framework seeks to unveil and point out the ways in which race has been, and continues to be, part of legal practices and, by extension, society (Delgado & Stefancic, 2012). Derrick Bell and Alan Freeman developed CRT and its central tenets because of their frustrations with critical legal studies (Delgado & Stefancic, 2000). Critical Race Theory is understood and applied through tenets that work to call out race and its semblances within society (Zamudio, Russell, Rios, & Bridgeman, 2011). Within the legal traditions of CRT, the tenets are as follow: Racism is Normal, Color Blindness, Differential Racialization, Interest Convergence, Counter Story-telling/Narrative, and Intersectionality and Anti-Essentialism (Delgado & Stefancic, 2012). We take up select tenets defined below to make sense of inclusion within a STEM-rich maker space while centering on the narratives of youth shared throughout.

The CRT tenet that racism is 'normal,' contends with the ways in which the normalizations of racism are entrenched within legal practice and functioning, and, as such, may go unnoticed (Delgado & Stefancic, 2012). Linked directly to the normalization of racism are objectivity and color-blindness. Color-Blindness, though utopic in its connotation, attempts to view practices and polices without considering the implications and history of race. However, this falls flat when considering legal histories and practices that were developed and implemented at a time when all people were not considered human, as well as how the real consequences of such practices that disproportionly affect communities racialized or were linked to anti-Blackness (Dumas, 2016). This also contributes to differential racialization pointing to the ways that not only are varying groups racialized differently, but also how the social construction of race affects some groups differently than others (Delgado & Stefancic, 2012). For the work of inclusion in STEM, this requires a mindfulness of the ways in which race and place matter with regard to making, STEM-rich experiences, and after-school environments.

The last tenet, Counter-Story/Narrative, is reflective of the use of testimony within trials. Counter-Story/Narrative seeks to disrupt dominant narratives that have either been passed off as true without ever being challenged or without acknowledging the different ways communities of color may live different realties (DeCuir & Dixon, 2004). Through not only sharing the narratives of youth within this work, but also co-authoring, we look to disrupt the dominant discourses that exclude Black girls from STEM and making, to see the ways in which their participation yields one of inclusivity and resistance – both socially and politically (Evans-Winter, 2007).

As such, we are deeply reflective of Ladson-Billings and Tate's (1995) Critical Race propositions to address the power of racism in education:

1) Race continues to play significant role in analyzing inequity in the US;
2) US society is based on property rights rather than human rights, and

3) The intersection of race and property is an analytic tool through which we can understand social inequity in and out of schools. (p.48)

Employing these concepts along with tenets that assess STEM and making call attention to forms of injustice reflected in practices that tend to be exclusionary. However, within this chapter, we present multiple co-authored, youth-centered narratives, that speak to the ways in which youth within a STEM-rich maker space have fostered inclusion and serve as a Critical Race praxis beyond exclusion. This practice is reflective of a resistance to dominant narratives of science and centers the fostering of community through the creation of a homeplace.

Homeplace

Historically, African American people believed that the construction of a homeplace, however fragile and tenuous (the slave hut, the wooden shack), had a radical political dimension. Despite the brutal reality of racial apartheid and of domination, one's homeplace was the only site where one could freely confront the issue of humanization, where one could resist. Black women resisted by making homes where all Black people could strive to be subjects, not objects, where we could be affirmed in our minds and hearts despite poverty, hardship, and deprivation, where we could restore to ourselves the dignity denied us on the outside in the public world. (hooks, 1990, p. 42)

bell hooks's description of homeplace captures a powerful view of how we might think about inclusion/exclusion in science education, especially for African American youth coming of age in lower socioeconomic (but rich socio-cultural) environments. Grounded in the struggle of Black women, homeplace is a powerful space for their families to build solidarity, away from, and in resistance to, the oppressions and violence inflicted by racialized and classed oppressions. It is also a place of healing, care, and love, as Black families (bound by my more than blood) share together a history of lives lived and worked towards an imagined future.

Since hooks wrote about homeplace in 1990, the idea has been taken up in Black Feminist works as a powerful approach for centering the humanizing and decolonizing practices and efforts of Black women (Morris A., 2017). Recently, scholars have taken up the intersectional dimensions of homeplace, calling attention to the importance of challenging gender and racial roles and identities ascribed to them (García, 2017), along with the experiences of migrant and immigrant families (Schmauch & Giritli-Nygren, 2014). As García (2017) explains, in the face of racism and sexism, Women of Color create homeplaces to question and critique oppression and develop counter-narratives as a buffer against the isolation and individualism that dominate White American culture. In a study of friendships among Black girls, homeplace has been described as a place that "ultimately enabled [the girls] to freely express their culturally based truths without fear of marginalization" (Goins, 2011, p. 531).

Homeplace is not a physical location, it is not a property; rather, it is a collective remembrance of lives lived and the wisdom, love, and resistance enacted in solidarity towards sustaining Black families (Jackson & Richardson, 2014). Families, in this sense, include extended families that come to know and rely on each other (Gouthro, 2000). That is, they bring together people who may or may not be "relatives" (as framed by dominant discourses). Homeplace acknowledges the relationalities within families without objectifying them. Relationships between parents and children go beyond children as property, or possessions of parents, to children and parents as members of a larger caring community of ongoing relationships, friendships, and sites for change (Morris A., 2017). Homeplace, then, is a communal space that draws strength from a common history and anguish, while also being a space of teaching and transformation; a place where the histories and collective knowledge of those who come before are central to its livelihood and where those experiences are brought to bear in ways that re-make science in more socially-just ways (Calabrese Barton & Osborne, 2001).

Homeplace emerges through care and solidarity, from which to "safeguard the rights of all . . . to be respected, and to be treated fairly" (Parsons, 2005, p. 26). Parsons (2005) describes care and solidarity as reciprocal, meaning that the act of caring involves a political effort to receive each other as one's own, and with a responsibility to "produce the best possible outcomes" (p. 27). This process necessarily involves creating spaces for all members to not only exist, but to be acknowledged and thrive, as opposed to only a select few benefiting from such a space. It also has a justice element as outlined earlier in our discussion of Critical Race Theory, where central to caring and solidarity is a critique of the "systemic, political, economic, and social structures that disproportionately appropriate opportunity according to race" along with "a commitment to challenge and alter them" (Parson, 2005, p. 26).

As such, homeplace reflects individual experiences and community memories that are passed down through the generations by way of legends, oral histories, and behavior (Montgomery, 2010; Naylor, 2005). More than simply weaving cultural ideas into what happens in education or other circles, homeplace enacts solidarity and care because they are places where cultural knowledge becomes "a thread of understanding and experiencing knowledge that is part of the fabric of how we think about schooling" (Gonzales, 2001, p. 653).

Homeplaces are, thus, built, enacted and sustained over time by practices that reflect these ideals of solidarity, resistance, teaching, care, and love with complexity and authenticity. Each one of these practices is always linked to remembrance and transformation. That is, practices are always critical and creative articulations of both historical and historicized experiences, and, therein, shapes how one comes to know the world. They each consider how the articulation of the historical brings with it a radical political dimension as it calls into question connections between position, power, and knowledge. The very act of articulation, in remembrance, politicizes experience, and the meaning of experience, while opening up spaces for critique and revision of those experiences and the world that helped shape them (Calabrese Barton & Osborne, 2001).

Such homeplaces are important in light of the harsh worlds of STEM, schooling, and society that African American girls navigate (Morris M., 2016). For Black girls who are not readily represented in narratives of STEM (Morton & Parson, 2018), having a home space in science is an act of resistance. More explicitly, considering the ways in which science serves as an example of Whiteness of property (Mensah & Jackson 2018), Black girls identifying with and practicing STEM is reflective of a critical race praxis (Roby, 2017). It is through the activist efforts of youth in after school science programs, such as GET (Green Energy Technologies) City (Calabrese Barton & Tan, 2018), where youth disrupt the dominant narratives of what science constitutes, who can do science, and why.

Homeplace and Homeplace-Making: How Youth Work Towards Inclusion

We consider the enactment of the practices detailed in the vignettes shared below as acts of homeplace-making. The following vignettes reflective of youth experiences in a STEM-rich after-school program serve as counter-narratives to the dominant narratives of the reasons why and how people may engage in STEM. Consider the following vignettes as examples of ways in which Critical Race Praxis is developed by youth, as well as making as a means of fostering homeplace work to encourage a more inclusive STEM, rather than an exclusive experience and practice.

Vignette 1: STEM without Limits

Over the summer the club's energy and vibrations are at an entirely different frequency than that of the regular academic year. During my summer hours at the club and extended time in the Teen Area, I (ReAnna) made a friend, Ari. Ari, a 16- going on 17-year-old girl was spending her first summer at the club. She entered the club space extremely reserved and would only speak if she wanted to. During her time in the Teen Zone, she and I worked on rolling magazine pages for an art project to take place weeks later. I would glue the sheets, while Ari would roll, using the pencil as a support. In between sessions, she and I would walk to lunch together and sit with one another during the daily symposium. She didn't enjoy the lunch on most days, so she had a stash of money at the club to use for hotdogs and bag of chips, each day. On Fridays, when dancing happened, Ari was one of the first to hit the floor and do the "shoot" dance. I could count on an embrace from Ari every day and knew she felt comfortable with me.

As we prepared for the summer camp, I spoke with Ari to let her know that I would not be in the Teen Zone as often, but that she could find me in the GET City room. GET City hosted two camps that year, one focused on the journeys and travels of food, and the other on robotics. The food camp involved a great deal of story-telling, interviewing, and investigation. When Ari shared with me that she wanted to participate in the camp, I was thrilled she wanted to leave the Teen Zone. After speaking with her grandmother, I sent permissions slips home with Ari and she enthusiastically returned them the next day.

During the camp, we started mornings with snack and conversation and then followed up with an activity. Most days, Ari was present for the morning snack, but would reconvene with our group after lunch. She worked in groups with youth and youth mentorsm and shared openly about her favorite foods, who prepared them, and her not-so-favorite foods. On the day we took a field trip to the local university, Ari's grandmother told me that Ari was so excited that she'd laid her clothes out earlier in the week and that night before the trip she barely slept. As a matter of fact, she was up by 4:00 AM on the day of our travels. During the trip, Ari took an active role in the making of ice cream and sharing with her peers. While the flavor was not quite her favorite, she was excited to share what she had leftover with Granny, the club matriarch.

Vignette 2: Bake Sale and Talent Show

I (Angie) had asked the group for other thoughts on inclusion. Sheree chimed in and said, "a bake sale!" When I asked her to say more about what she was thinking, she said, "We should have a bake sale. It would help everyone feel included because everyone can work together. You all can buy the food so we have the ingredients, then we could bake the things."

Sheree's conversation developed into an animated discussion about the need for a bake sale. They wished for anyone in their STEM club to participate and came up with ideas for different roles for everyone to be able to participate, even kids who don't like baking, or might have expertise in different areas. They included the idea that they could have a "bake challenge" (similar to a popular Bake Challenge Shows on television) that would have options for participating in the challenge if they wanted to, or for people just to bake if they did not want to. As one of the youths explained, "We could have our own competition. But it wouldn't be like on TV. Anyone who wants to bake something can and if you don't, you can just be there and bake. If you want to compete you can but you can also just bake."

When I had asked who was interested in planning the baking session, everyone raised their hands. When I then suggested that we could use time at our next session (the following week, which was the Tuesday before Thanksgiving), several youth chimed in that they wanted to plan it today, as they wished to bake on that Tuesday. As one of the youth succinctly put it, "If we all baked on Tuesday, we could all have something for a Thanksgiving dinner."

This idea was then followed by another animated discussion on a GET City Talent Show. Chloe suggested that "another thing we could do is a talent show" when I asked if there were more ideas about inclusion. She said it would be a "GET City Talent Show, where you can show what you learned. You can act, sing or dance or whatever." This was met with immediate enthusiasm from others, and youth were pitching in ideas at once, "A show!" "A skit!" "You can dance your ideas!" When one of the GET City mentors, Sarah, chimed in that "You guys bring some awesome talent!" Chloe agreed, and expanded upon her idea, "We should do it near the end of GET City. Each person can do something that shows what you learned. You can do it however you want. You can teach what you learned to others. They will like it because it will be enjoyable."

Vignette 3: A Place for Home in STEM

The idea that a GET City do it yourself (DIY) baking competition would have everyone working together, include multiple roles/jobs that would draw upon everyone's different expertise, and would provide food for Thanksgiving, speaks to multiple aspects of inclusion we often strive to foster among our youth. That same day, I had been in the club office, and had observed two of the staff members going over the Thanksgiving bag list. Over 300 families served by the club would be getting Thanksgiving bags full of foods to help their families prepare special meals.

That cooking, dance, acting, singing and so forth could be central to engaging in STEM on multiple levels relational to these youth also speaks to how they wish to see themselves, and have others see them, as STEM people. Furthermore, the youth purposefully seeking to create spaces for themselves, and their peers, to thrive in STEM given the various interests and strengths they bring to the collective learning experience speaks to powerful forms of solidarity and care. Departing from traditional notions or images of STEM, this served as a means of disruption and redistribution of power with regards to naming and creating one's own experiences.

When the group of youth were discussing inclusion, Louise stated that one thing that made her feel included was when people noticed her in positive ways. She pointed out that in the previous session, I (Angie) had noticed her sewing skills, and pointed out how good they were, she went on to disclose that she remembered she could sew at the YAC (Young Archaeologists Club) camp the previous summer. She said that an auntie had taught her how to sew. She said that what made that really important to her was that later in the session we had done two things: First, we had asked the youth in the room to raise their hands if they felt like they were good at sewing. As she stated, "Sometimes y'all be like 'who is a pro at this?' and y'all be like 'look Aleya is pro!' and when you guys talk about that one specific person who is an expert, then that helps." Louise, then, said it was important for kids to feel like experts because school usually does the opposite. "It doesn't matter if you are smart or not, usually it's just 'who doesn't get it' and 'who is making too much noise' or whatever. It's like the opposite kind of attention. The opposite of inclusion."

Discussion

Among our collective work in science and STEM education, we see youth as actively engaged in co-constructing homeplaces in ways that allow them to engage in STEM while reimagining who and what STEM and making are for. For the youth, as for bell hooks and others, their homeplace – in this case, GET City – is a place of remembrance, solidarity, and resistance as they seek to learn and become in STEM in ways that matter to them and their communities. GET City has become more than a place to make or do things in STEM, but one of care and love. In GET City, they seek to build each other up, even as the worlds of STEM and schooling often strive to tear them down. GET City became, and continues to be, a place for teaching, imagining, and a means of transformation as these youth seek to share their own constructions of STEM while inviting families and communities to do so as well.

Our youth's experiences in this after-school STEM-rich maker space speak to the ways in which Black youth take on STEM and make it their own. In the process of doing so, the youth take ownership and authority in naming their experiences and sharing their skills in ways that are meaningful for them. Their work toward disrupting and reconstructing power in STEM takes to task the ways in which Whiteness as property – or, in this case, science as property – can be deconstructed. Additionally, it is reflective of the Black feminist experiences, which work to point and name one's experiences on their own terms. Doing this work while not alienating peers due to differences in ability or access is also reflective of the African philosophy, *ubuntu*, 'I am because we are' (Waghid, 2018).

At the close of Ari's vignette, she is pictured with a colleague, as well as with the ice cream she and the youth made. The collective support of Ari in GET City by mentors, as well as fellow members, made Ari's experience in GET City one that challenged how youth participate in after school science and STEM when they are invited. As scholars continue to become more critical of the ways in which ability is taken up within discourse, it is especially meaningful to consider what inclusion looks like large-scale, or even at the different grain-sizes, one that questions how we make sense of ability with regard to communication, physicality, and more.

In the Bake Challenge Show vignette, we are reminded of the brilliant ways in which youth create opportunities and spaces for everybody to be present, and to share. This work is reflective of a praxis that acknowledges that while everyone may not have the same talents or skills, they can still take part and be included in the process. As a Critical Race Praxis, what youth offer is a call to reconsider the ways in which the formalization of science may exclude participants because they don't behave or perform science in the most traditional sense. This requires seeing, hearing and listening to the multiple experiences and perspectives offered by youth as they navigate and re-create science for themselves. This act of resistance is necessary if science and STEM are truly to be practice-based disciplines of solidarity that foster senses of home-space.

The final vignette, which takes up noticing through Louise's sharing makes apparent the types of things she would like to be noticed for – see 'her.' This is important as dominant narratives regarding Black girls and their positions in classroom oftentimes demonize their behaviors and existence (Evans-Winters & Esposito, 2010). Being acknowledged as an expert or having the influence of familial experts is important to the sustaining of homeplace. Which experts are named, pictured, or recalled, is meaningful. What we can learn from this as a field is to consider how we center those who are not normally named or included as we work to make science, making, and STEM-rich learning embody homeplace.

Through the construction of this chapter, our co-authors have shown us how we can view science and STEM education as a constructive place in which the enterprise of science can be rethought and "science" can be placed in a position as a tool to be leveraged toward enacting societal change for the better of those that are learning it, as well as their communities. This, in turn, means a reconstruction of both "homeplace" and the "harsh world" that is science itself – reconstructing the spaces that youth occupy when learning STEM, science, and making in more socially-just ways. Youth engaging in Critical Race Praxis, alongside adult peers and their teachers, presents a special set of challenges. However, the relationships developed and fostered while co-learning and growing together sustains hope and love, which are certainly requirements and catalysts for such critical work. As we continue to engage and promote STEM and making in ways that seek to disrupt the dominant discourses of STEM and science education, we channel Derrick Bell (1995), whose firm stance of racial realism was paralleled with a tenacity to imagine and work towards a more equitable, just, and inclusive world for all learners.

REFERENCES

Bell, D. A. (1995). Who's afraid of critical race theory. U. Ill. L. Rev., 893.

Calabrese Barton, A. & Osborne, M. (2001). Homeplace and the Harshworld: A feminist re-reading of science and teaching students in poverty. Journal of Curriculum Theorizing, 17, 131-144.

Calabrese Barton, A., & Tan, E. (2018). A longitudinal study of equity-oriented STEM-rich making among youth from historically marginalized communities. American Educational Research Journal, 55, 761-800. doi: 0002831218758668.

Crenshaw, K., Gotanda, N., Peller, G. & Thomas, K. (1995). Introduction. In K. Crenshaw, N. Gotanda, G. Peller & K. Thomas (Eds.), Critical race theory: The key writings that formed the movement (pp. xiii – xxxii). New York: The New Press.

Casey Tieken, M. (2010). Editor's Review. Belonging: A Culture of Place-by bell hooks. Harvard Educational Review, 80(2), 275.

DeCuir, J. T., & Dixson, A. D. (2004). "So when it comes out, they aren't that surprised that it is there": Using critical race theory as a tool of analysis of race and racism in education. Educational Researcher, 33(5), 26-31.

Delgado, R. & Stefancic, J. (Eds.) (2000). *Critical race theory: The cutting edge*. Chicago: Temple University Press.

Delgado, R., & Stefancic, J. (2012). *Critical race theory: An introduction*. NYU Press.

Dumas, M. J. (2016). Against the dark: Antiblackness in education policy and discourse. *Theory into Practice*, 55(1), 11-19.

Evans-Winters, V. (2007). 11. Urban African American female students and educational resiliency. *Counterpoints*, 306, 167-178.

Evans-Winters, V. E., & Esposito, J. (2010). Other people's daughters: Critical race feminism and Black girls' education. *Educational Foundations*, 24, 11-24.

García, M. G. (2017). Creating a homeplace: Young Latinas constructing feminista identities in the context of a single-sex Catholic school. *The High School Journal*, 101(1), 27-48.

Goins, M. N. (2011). Playing with dialectics: Black female friendship groups as a homeplace. *Communication Studies*, 62, 531-546.

Gonzales, F. (2001). Haciendo que hacer - cultivating a Mestiza worldview and academic achievement: braiding cultural knowledge into educational research, policy, practice. *International Journal of Qualitative Studies in Education* 14, 641-656.

Gouthro, P. (2000). Globalization, civil society, and the homeplace. *Convergence*, 33(1–2), 57–77.

hooks, b. (1990). *Yearning: Race, gender, and cultural politics*. Cambridge, MA: South End Press.

hooks, b. (2009). *Belonging. A culture of place*. New York: Routledge.

Jackson II, R. L., & Richardson, E. B. (2014). *Understanding African American rhetoric: Classical origins to contemporary innovations*. Routledge.

Ladson-Billings, G., & Tate IV, W. F. (1995). Toward a critical race theory of education. *Teachers College Record*, 97(1), 47-68.

Mensah, F. M., & Jackson, I. (2018). Whiteness as property in science teacher education. *Teachers College Record*, 120(1), 1-38

Montgomery, M. L. (2010). *The fiction of Gloria Naylor: Houses and spaces of resistance*. Univ. of Tennessee Press.

Morris, A. (2017). Materialities of homeplace. *Historical Archaeology*, 51(1), 28-42.

Morris, M. (2016). *Pushout: The criminalization of Black girls in schools*. New Press, The.

Morton, T. R., & Parsons, E. C. (2018). # BlackGirlMagic: The identity conceptualization of Black women in undergraduate STEM education. *Science Education*, 102, 1363-1393.

Naylor, G. (2005). *The women of Brewster place*. Penguin.

Parsons, E. C. (2005). From caring as a relation to culturally relevant caring: A White teacher's bridge to Black students. *Equity & Excellence in Education*, 38(1), 25-34.

Roby, R.S. (2017). Black girl magic in science: A critical race narrative of Black women in science PhD programs (Doctoral dissertation, The University of Texas at San Antonio).

Schmauch, U., & Giritli Nygren, K. (2014). The hidden boundaries of everyday places: Migrant women, homeplace and the spatial practices of a small Swedish town. *ACME: An International E-Journal for Critical Geographies*, 13, 372-393.

Waghid, Y. (2018). On the educational potential of ubuntu. In E. J. Takyi-Amoako & N. Thérèse Assié-Lumumba (Eds.), *Re-visioning education in Africa* (pp. 55-65). Palgrave Macmillan, Cham.

Zamudio, M., Russell, C., Rios, F., & Bridgeman, J. L. (2011). *Critical race theory matters: Education and ideology*. Routledge.

Chapter 9

QUEERING EXCLUSION

A Post-Oppositional Meditation

ANALOUISE KEATING

> The whole time growing up I felt that I was not of this earth. An alien from another planet – I'd been dropped on my mother's lap. But for what purpose? (Anzaldúa, 1981, p. 222)

In "La Prieta," her early autohistoria, Gloria Anzaldúa narrates her experiences with exclusion, experiences that alienated her so profoundly from her surroundings that she felt inhuman, nonhuman – like "[a]n alien from another planet." A Brown-skinned, Spanish-speaking girl of Mexican descent, born and raised in the Rio Grande Valley of south Texas (a state not known for its progressive views, to say the least), she was punished in kindergarten for her inability to speak English and experienced multiple, intersecting forms of race-, class-, and gender-based oppression throughout her childhood.[1] Because she was very smart, her Anglo (White) teachers often singled her out from the other Mexican-American children, treating her like a rare exception and, thus, inadvertently leaving her even more alienated, isolated, and alone – unable to fit in with the Anglos, and subsequently also unable to fit in with the Mexican-American kids.

Her physiological differences further intensified the young Anzaldúa's feelings of alienation and exclusion. She had a rare hormonal condition that led to early menstruation and full puberty at the age of six, when she developed breasts and began menstruating each month. She grew to four feet eleven inches, thus towering over the other children her age. Her mother bound her "budding breasts" and helped her to hide evidence of her menstruation from her siblings, but these actions – though well-intended – made Anzaldúa feel even more excluded from childhood norms. These physiologically based differences affected her profoundly, shaping her self-definition while isolating her from family and friends:

> ...in the eyes of others I saw myself reflected as "strange," "abnormal," "QUEER." I saw no other reflection. Helpless to change that image, I retreated into books and solitude and kept away from others. (1981, p. 222)

I will return to Anzaldúa's association of queerness with exclusion (and her expansive use of the word "queer," years before it entered academia's vocabulary and before "queer theory" became a cutting-edge field) later in the chapter. Here I want to emphasize how deeply estranged and excluded the young Anzaldúa felt. Indeed, as my epigraph suggests, she viewed herself as so different – so extremely excluded from conventional human norms – that she felt entirely nonhuman; like a member of another species; like an alien from another planet.

And this, of course, is how exclusion functions: In conjunction with externally imposed norms (which are, too often, internalized by those who bear the brunt of its pressure and isolating maneuvers), it marks us as different. Here difference is not merely a categorical marker, it is defined hierarchically – as inferior to the unmarked norm – and isolates us from our social setting and other people. If you're excluded, you're cast out, you don't belong, you're an Other, an outsider, one of them. Marked as DIFFERENT. OTHER. ALIEN. All too often, the exclusion becomes debilitating; it erodes our self-confidence, stifles our intuitive creativity, and, in addition, prevents us from achieving our goals – preventing us from living out our lives to their fullest. Exclusion functions energetically, as well. When we're excluded, we sense the rejection; it seeps insidiously into the skin, deep into our tissues: You're not one of us; you're not wanted. These voices imposed onto us from outside of us haunt our psyches.

Exclusion has its source, at least partially, in an oppositional, Cartesian-based epistemology – a dichotomous mode of thought that divides reality into two distinct, hierarchically ranked parts (e.g., mind/body, man/woman, reason/emotion, us/them). The product of European Enlightenment philosophy, oppositionality enacts an either/or worldview that relies almost entirely on rational thought, linear logic, and boundaried categories, thus under-valuing imagination, intuition, and contradiction. Oppositional thought manifests itself as a set of divide-and-conquer beliefs and us-versus-them frameworks that separate the world into discrete parts which are then analyzed, compared, and ranked, creating rigid hierarchies. Applied to human beings (as it typically is in most, if not all, western cultures), oppositional thought categorizes and labels us, treating people differently depending on where they are ranked. In oppositional thought, there are always "winners" and losers;" the winner takes all, and the loser leaves empty-handed – kind of like the way U.S. "democracy" functions in national and state elections.

Generated through these oppositional dynamics, exclusion reproduces and intensifies us-versus-them frameworks, creating more and more divisions among us by virtue of its foundational purpose and nature. Each exclusionary tale breeds additional exclusions, and the energy continues, cycling more boldly with each new exclusionary act. Sometimes the excluded join together, seeking power to challenge those who excluded them. Elevating themselves, they speak with a hard-won moral authority as they carve up new differences and create new hierarchies, subordinating and excluding those who excluded them. In short, they flip the script. At times, this flipped script becomes even more convoluted, as we further internalize oppositional energies and use them against each other, creating new divisions within ourselves, among our allies.[2] And so, oppositionality gains more energy, creates more us-against-them situations and dynamics that spiral onward, almost endlessly. Anzaldúa exposes this dynamic in "La Prieta":

> The violence against us, the violence within us, aroused like a rabid dog. Adrenaline-filled bodies, we bring home the anger and the violence we meet on the street and turn it against each other. We sic the rabid dog on each other and on ourselves. The black moods of alienation descend, the bridges we've extended out to each other crumble. We put the walls back up between us. (1981, p. 229, her italics)

But how do we escape these oppositional dynamics? How do we respond to exclusion in healthy, self-nurturing ways that foster loving, diverse communities? How do we create and enact alternative forms of thinking and being that don't inadvertently reinstate oppressive norms (or create new, equally oppressive norms)?

In what follows, I draw from Anzaldúa's identity-related theories to address these questions. More specifically, I examine three post-oppositional tactics she employs: (1) Questioning status-quo identity categories; (2) Redefining human identity in broader, more expansive terms that exceed the status-quo; and (3) Creating relational, invitational coalitions. I describe these tactics as post-oppositional because they neither entirely embrace nor fully reject oppositional thinking but instead glean lessons from it. As I have explained in *Transformation Now! Toward a Post-Oppositional Politics of Change*, post-oppositionality represents relational approaches to knowledge production, identity formation, social interactions, and transformation that borrow from, but do not become limited by or trapped within, oppositional thought and action.

Driven by my desire to discover and (when necessary) create connections among apparently disparate people and things, I developed the theory and practice of post-oppositionality to avoid the limitations in oppositional thought in innovative ways, specifically ways that don't simply (and ironically) oppose oppositionality by rejecting it. Applied to questions of exclusion, post-oppositional perspectives transform conventional self/other, us-versus-them divisions into complex new narratives that embrace contradiction, paradox, and transformation. Applied to questions of pedagogy or education more broadly, post-oppositionality offers a fresh approach to creating inclusive classroom communities while fostering a 21st-century planetary citizenship.

Post-Oppositional Tactic #1: Questioning Status-Quo Identity Categories

We see the first tactic at work in a section of "La Prieta" titled, "Who Are My People?," where Anzaldúa uses her personal experiences to question the existing social identity categories – conventional definitions of race, gender, and so on. As an activist, she interacted with numerous social-justice groups; however, each progressive group tried to impose its own oppositional identity, definitions, and expectations on all members of their group – including Anzaldúa. She refuses these imposed definitions, naming herself a complex mediator:

> I am a wind-swayed bridge, a crossroads inhabited by whirlwinds. Gloria, the facilitator, Gloria the mediator, straddling the walls between abysses. "Your allegiance is to La Raza, the Chicano movement," say the members of my race. "Your allegiance is to the Third World," say my Black and Asian friends. "Your allegiance is to your gender, to women," say the feminists. Then there's my allegiance to the Gay movement, to the socialist revolution, to the New Age, to magic and the occult. And there's my affinity to literature, to the world of the artist. What am I? A third world lesbian feminist with Marxist and mystic leanings. (1981, p. 228, her italics)

Anzaldúa wrote "La Prieta" from 1979 to 1980 – a time when many social justice groups were deeply invested in various forms of separatism and nationalist politics. Her experience reminds us that even progressive groups committed to social change can practice exclusionary dynamics. Significantly, Anzaldúa resists these dynamics without rejecting (excluding) the various movements or the activists within these movements.

Rather than exclusively highlight one specific component of her identity by aligning herself with only one group, Anzaldúa defines herself more broadly, in terms enabling her to affirm her divergent identities – despite the apparent paradox this affirmation involves. She offers an inclusive response to her allies' seemingly self-imposed exclusionary demands:

> You say my name is ambivalence? Think of me as Shiva, a many-armed and legged body with one foot on Brown soil, one on White, one in straight society, one in the gay world, the man's world, the women's, one limb in the literary world, another in the working class, the socialist, and the occult worlds. A sort of spider woman hanging by one thin strand of web. Who, me confused? Ambivalent? Not so. Only your labels split me. (1981, p. 228)

In this passage, Anzaldúa resists the existing social script by demonstrating its limitations in describing the multiplicities of her personhood and identity. Although members of the various specific groups to which she could be said to belong accused her of disloyalty and indecision, demanding that she align herself exclusively with one group, she denies these accusations by demonstrating that the problem is with the groups themselves: they have defined themselves in limited ways, based on social scripts established by the hierarchical system that oppresses them. Their thinking remains locked in the status quo. By exposing the limitations in narrow definitions of group identity, Anzaldúa turns the mirror back on those who unthinkingly use these externally imposed identities to exclude.

I have used this tactic as an educator, especially in conversations with administrators, academics, or other sources of (hierarchical) authority, which has led me to understand this tactic in pragmatic ways. For example, I have often been asked (i.e., required) to create courses or units that follow conventional categories of socially inscribed human identities – for instance, a course on Chicana literature, a unit on Black history, a section on women's issues, and so on. Rather than openly critiquing, resisting, or rejecting this request, I question the specific labels and explore the boundaries of the categories themselves. At times, I ask these questions immediately, in order to create more flexible courses, units, and so on. At other times, I accede to my superiors' request but structure the course or section in ways designed to question the labels, thus inviting my students to examine (and begin questioning) status-quo human categories. Through this tactic, I reframe the pedagogical importance of actively disrupting who and for reasons humans define ourselves through stationary labels; in turn, my students are asked to consider themselves as subjects in this process – as makers of their own realities – which aligns with the second tactic.

Post-Oppositional Tactic #2: Redefining Human Identity In Expansive Terms

This second tactic flows almost seamlessly from the first. After all, it's not enough simply to question existing social scripts and identity labels; we must also offer effective alternatives in their place. Throughout her work, Anzaldúa develops innovative configurations that expand conventional conceptions of human identity. Indeed, we could say that she fundamentally redefines what it means to be human, both in her writing style and rhetoric moves. For example, in one of her earliest poems, "The coming of el mundo surdo," she describes herself in terms that go beyond conventional definitions of human identity: "I am the unmoving center / Within my skin all races / sexes / all trees grasses / cows and snails" (36).

She dissolves conventional racial and sexual divisions, as well as the division between human and nonhuman life, by locating them all within herself. In so doing, she completely bypasses U.S. racial classifications that rely on the belief in racial purity and rigid boundaries dividing each 'race' from all others. Anzaldúa resists these stark divisions, positing in their stead a web of radical inter-special, ecological interconnectedness that does not deny distinct races but rather redefines each race as parts of a larger whole. Similarly, in an unpublished collection of early notes and partial drafts titled "Notes on El Mundo Surdo Essay," she writes that "at the group level I've always felt or wanted to feel that all races are organs in the giant organism, life, and that individuals are cells in these organs." It is through this turn within her argument where she finds a new way of identifying herself, as well as a method to break down those boundaries that have excluded her in the past.

I attribute Anzaldúa's expansive definitions of human and nonhuman life to her worldview – which I describe as a metaphysics of interconnectedness. She replaces conventional Judeo-Christian descriptions of nature as fallen and separated from the divine with an indigenous-inflected worldview that defines nature – including humanity – as innately sacred. As she asserts in Light in the Dark/Luz en lo oscuro: Rewriting Identity, Spirituality, Reality:

> You stand on tierra sagrada – nature is alive and conscious; the world is
> ensouled. You lift your head to the sky, to the wingspread of pelicans, the

stark green of trees, the wind sighing through their branches. You discern faces in the rocks and allow them to see you. You become reacquainted with a reality called spirit, a presence, force, power, and energy within and without. Spirit infuses all that exists – organic and inorganic – transcending the categories and concepts that govern your perception of material reality. Spirit speaks through your mouth, listens through your ears, sees through your eyes, touches with your hands. (2015, p. 138)

In Anzaldúa's holistic worldview, everything that exists is infused with spirit and thus sacred, divine, and interconnected. This relational worldview enables her to blur the boundaries between apparently discrete things.

To be sure, most educators can't talk openly with our students about apparently nonsecular topics like spirit, divine selfhood, or innate divinity. However, we can learn from Anzaldúa's radically expansive approach and glean insights, tactics, and strategies to adopt and revise for our specific contexts (contexts that include students, region, school, subject area, etc.). For example, I have challenged the anthropocentric, myopic focus on the human and the assumption that human beings are radically, starkly different from (and superior to) all other life forms by incorporating indigenous creation narratives into some of the courses I teach. In addition to demonstrating types of shared consciousness between human and nonhuman animals, these narratives use kinship terms ("brother," "sister," etc.) when referring to nonhuman animals, plants, stones, and so on, thus underscoring connections among us. And, when relevant to the course topics, I challenge conventional assumptions that racial categories are permanent, unchanging, and natural by historicizing race and discussing the invention of White people.[3] Within this push toward reframing humanity and its existence in relation to the larger ecology of the Earth, I intend to help my students also face their own stories of who they are and who they can become, and why. Through this process, there are some that see the value in such as metacognitive process and others who don't, which is where the third tactic comes into play.

Post-Oppositional Tactic #3: Creating Relational, Invitational Coalitions

Questioning status-quo identities and offering more expansive definitions of human identities in their place leads to the third tactic: creating relational coalitions that are spacious enough to lovingly affirm and embrace the differences among us. These relational coalitions become possible when we no longer view identity as restrictive, as bounded by impermeable walls. Look for instance at Anzaldúa's inclusive community-building in the "El Mundo Surdo" reading series and writing workshops she initiated in the late 1970s. While grounded in women-of-colors perspectives, the reading series and workshops were open to progressive people of any identity. Similarly, in her 2001 co-edited collection, *this bridge we call home: radical visions of transformation*, she invites people of any gender, race, sexuality, and so on to contribute. As she explains in her preface,

> By including women and men of different "races," nationalities, classes, sexualities, genders, and ages we complicate the debates within feminist theory both inside and outside the academy and inside and outside the U.S. Gathering people from many geographies in a multicultural approach is a mark of inclusivity, increased consciousness and dialogue. This inclusivity reflects the hybrid quality of our lives and identities – todas somos nos/otras. Living in multicultural communities and the complexities of our age demand we develop a perspective that takes into account the whole planet. (p. 3)

Anzaldúa's inclusiveness is particularly important in the context of *this bridge we call home* because this book is in direct dialogue with her earlier co-edited collection, *This Bridge Called My Back: Writings by Radical Women of Color*.

As the title suggests, *This Bridge Called My Back* consists exclusively of writings by self-identified women of colors. Often in direct dialogue with White-raced feminists, *This Bridge Called My Back* is a foundational feminist text that has played an almost-sacred role for many women of colors. By opening the conversation to people who are not women of colors, Anzaldúa makes a radically inclusive gesture that emphasizes the value of woman-of-colors theories and experiences for all readers regardless of gender, race, and so on. In effect, the relational and fluid arguments within her writings become embodied within her decisions within this publication series to represent the practice she preached.

Relational coalitions do not ignore the differences among us but instead redefine them as interdependent and nonhierarchical. This relational approach to difference can sidestep oppositional thought's hierarchical rankings. Thus, in the preface to *this bridge we call home* Anzaldúa does not permit her desire for inclusive, planetary-wide identities to erase or ignore the embodied, socially inscribed differences among us. As she explains:

Our goal is not to use differences to separate us from others, but neither is it to gloss over them. Many of us identify with groups and social positions not limited to our ethnic, racial, religious, class, gender, or national classifications. Though most people self-define by what they exclude, we define who we are by what we include—what I call the new tribalism. (2002, p. 3)

I want to underscore the radical implications of Anzaldúa's suggestion that we reconfigure identity by defining ourselves inclusively. Typically, we self-define through a process of exclusion: I define who I am by telling you who I am not. If I self-define as queer, for instance, I do so by stating that I am not heterosexual. If I self-define as a woman of color, I imply that I'm neither White nor a man. And so on, and on, and on. Anzaldúa offers a far different approach, one that exceeds social location.

Applied to education, this inclusive approach to identity facilitates the development of innovative configurations for study. Rather than simply accepting conventional categories, we can be creative and mix things up. In more practical terms, when I'm teaching U.S. literature, I no longer divide units into categories based on specific ethnic/racial groups but instead use alternative groupings – themes, genres, regions, and so on. I underscore the relevance of every text we read for all students, and I encourage students (regardless of how they self-define) to question conventional literary groupings: African-American literature, Chicana/o literature, Asian-American literature, and so on. For example, while studying African-American literature, I encourage students to investigate the various ways "American literature" is defined: What counts as literature? How is "American" defined? Prior to this investigation, I ensure that students have a solid literary, theoretical and historical foundation, so that they can understand the status-quo definitions that have restrictively shaped literary categories and, therein, our discussions about this radical change in defining yourself and others does not push students away and, rather, welcomes them into that space to explore these ideas together – welcoming them into a Queered space to discuss exclusion.

El Mundo Zurdo's Queer Space

Anzaldúa's theory of El Mundo Zurdo illustrates her inclusionary dynamic. Indeed, even the name – which translates into English as "The Left-Handed World (i.e., the world Anzaldúa associates with the feminine, intuition, and spirit) – points to her expansive desire to embrace and affirm that which is typically rejected. Although one of her earliest theories, Anzaldúa continued developing El Mundo Zurdo throughout her career, giving it a variety of ethical, epistemological, and aesthetic dimensions. For the purposes of this chapter, I define El Mundo Zurdo as a visionary, post-oppositional approach to identity, alliance-making, and social change that uses contradiction and relational differences to develop new forms of community – a queer sociality driven by radical, contradictory love.[4] I describe El Mundo Zurdo as visionary because of its generous worldview – its grounding in a metaphysics of interconnectedness (as described in the previous section) that ensures a universal basic goodness or spirit infusing all that exists. Applied to interpersonal human relationships, this worldview invites us to initiate alliances based on commonalities. I describe El Mundo Zurdo as post-oppositional because it replaces oppositional divide-and-conquer thinking with imagination, intuition, and other types of non-Cartesian embodied thought, which inevitably lead to discussions on why these isolating labels were created in the first place and how they are perpetuated. Moreover, the theory itself emerged post-oppositionally: Anzaldúa developed this visionary theory by responding thoughtfully (rather than by reacting oppositionally) to the oppositional demands and other forms of exclusion she experienced throughout her life.

Anzaldúa discusses this radically inclusive theory in the conclusion to "La Prieta," in the section titled "El Mundo Zurdo (The Left-handed World)," where she responds to the various forms of exclusion she experienced both from the dominating U.S. culture and from progressive social justice groups. As I explained earlier in this chapter, Anzaldúa does not respond oppositionally by replicating these exclusionary dynamics; instead, she responds queerly (by which I mean 'out of the norm' and 'expansively') and replaces them with a generous, inclusionary approach that creates an intellectual-emotional space of radical acceptance. As she explains, "Both cultures deny me a place in their universe. Between them and among others, I build my own universe, El Mundo Zurdo. I belong to myself and not to any one people" (1981, p. 232). This statement offers a reply to the separatist groups demanding Anzaldúa's total loyalty. Anzaldúa does not condemn exclusion as unjust; nor does she react by rejecting those who rejected her as "abnormal." Instead, she enacts a relational approach that acknowledges, questions, and transforms exclusion in ways that support the building of bridges, the charting of radical coalition, and questioning the very nature of exclusion.

Indeed, Anzaldúa queers exclusion by embracing its potential to include. More specifically, she uses our experiences of being excluded to create El Mundo Zurdo – her visionary, inclusive model of coalition-building and alliance-making. In this context, Anzaldúan queering represents a post-oppositional epistemology and ethics that embraces multiplicity and, thus, transforms divergent concepts. As in her earlier self-description as "'strange,' 'abnormal,' 'QUEER,'" where her identity as queer includes more than sexuality, Anzaldúa responds expansively to exclusionary energies. With El Mundo Zurdo she redefines exclusion as itself a form of inclusion and then uses this queer inclusiveness to develop a new type of belonging. She takes exclusion's opposite (inclusion) and uses it to redefine exclusion as an invitation to be included. Put differently, she reminds us that exclusion is, itself, a concept that resonates with many people: The experience of being excluded from some form of socially defined norm and the concurrent sense of being an outsider, a misfit, an outcast. Instead of rejecting ourselves because of our outcast status, we embrace it – loving ourselves and bonding with others. In this way, she asserts a new narrative toward living through exclusion:

> We are the queer groups, the people that don't belong anywhere, not in the dominant world nor completely within our own respective cultures. Combined we cover so many oppressions. But the overwhelming oppression is the collective fact that we do not fit, and because we do not fit, we are a threat. (1981, p. 233, her italics)

As this statement indicates, Anzaldúa's Left-Handed World does not require sameness. Las Zurdistx (those of us living El Mundo Zurdo) have experienced nonbelonging and exclusion for a variety of reasons, many of which come from beyond ourselves but end up imposing their narratives of deficit in our psyches. We have experienced different oppressions, and we self-define in a variety of ways; often we have different politics, solutions, and beliefs. But by queering these differences – by viewing them relationally, rather than oppositionally – we avoid defining them in mutually exclusive, oppositional ways. Indeed, "these different affinities are not opposed to each other. In El Mundo Zurdo I with my own affinities and my people with theirs can live together and transform the planet" (233). Through this frame, it's the variety of differences, co-existing, merging, mingling, that makes El Mundo Zurdo so productive – a queer sociality.

My goal as an educator is to build El Mundo Zurdo – to transform exclusion into innovative learning communities that invite students to explore differences relationally rather than oppositionally. I do so by focusing first on commonalities, defined not as identical sameness but rather as complex points of possible connection that include difference. When I begin with commonalities, my students remain more open to learning about concepts, worldviews, and peoples different from themselves. Investigating commonalities invites them to move closer to their "others," to learn without judging, to investigate without ranking. It is through this process of finding yourself in another person where my students start to develop a curiosity for, and hopefully sustained love toward, people different from them – as represented demographically, philosophically, and politically. In turn, I am left with the following question: How can we continue this post-oppositional work of queering exclusion – if we so chose to do so?

To summarize, Anzaldúa enacts three steps that we can borrow, build on, revise, and enact in our struggles with exclusionary systems. First, she questions status-quo stories – the existing social scripts, identity labels, and cultural assumptions (even those held by progressive groups). Second, she creates broader, more inclusive identities beginning with her own self-definition and uses this broader, more expansive approach to redefine all human and nonhuman life as interconnected and ecologically bound to one another. Third, she uses this radically inclusive identity to create relational, invitational coalitions that honor individual differences and group social identities while also locating them in relation to a co-existing commonality – what, near the end of her life she describes as "a category of identity wider than any social position or racial label" (2015, p. 138).

Anzaldúa calls us to a new type of inclusive politics, a radically queer politics that embraces relational difference by shifting the focus to larger goals and visions and it my wish that we start the process of taking up this coalition-building – this relational identifying of similarities that honor difference through inclusion – and, in turn, change the world for the better by pedagogically employing these tactics both in our teaching and our personal lives. Without which, we will continue to sustain the us-versus-them mentality that divides and conquers our spirit, our polity, and our personal sense of Self as valuable by virtue of its creation, rather than what category you fall into upon birth.

REFERENCES

Anzaldúa, G. E. (1981). La Prieta. In C. Moraga & G. Anzaldúa (Eds.), *This bridge called my back: Writings by radical women of color* (pp. 198-209), New York: Kitchen Table: Women of Color Press.

Anzaldúa, G. E. (2002). (Un)natural bridges, (Un)safe spaces. In G. Anzaldúa & A. Keating (Eds.) *this bridge we call home: radical visions for transformation* (pp. 1-5). New York Routledge.

Anzaldúa, G. E. (2009). The coming of el mundo surdo. In A. Keating (Ed.), The Gloria Anzaldúa reader (pp. 36-37), Duke University Press. Doi: 10.1215/9780822391272-009

Anzaldúa, G. E. (2015). *Light in the dark/Luz en lo oscuro: Rewriting identity, spirituality, reality.* (Edited by A. Keating). Duke University Press.

Anzaldúa, G. E. (n.d.). *Notes on El Mundo Surdo Essay.* Box 61, Folder 18. Gloria Evangelina Anzaldúa Papers. Nettie Lee Benson Latin American Collection, University of Texas, Austin.

Anzaldúa, G. E., & AnaLouise Keating (Eds.) (2002). *this bridge we call home: radical visions for transformation.* Routledge,

Bacchetta, P. (May, 2018). *Wild Tongues/Transnational Crossings: Reflections on Translating Anzaldúa into French*, El Mundo Zurdo Conference, San Antonio, TX.

Keating, A. (2000). *Interviews/Entrevistas: Gloria E. Anzaldua.* New York: Routledge.

Keating, A. (2007). *Teaching transformation: Transcultural classroom dialogues.* Springer.

Keating, A. (2013). *Transformation now!: Toward a post-oppositional politics of change.* University of Illinois Press.

notes

2. I discuss this process at greater length in *Transformation Now! Towards a Post-Oppositional Politics of Change.*

3. For extensive examples of how I incorporate these strategies into my teaching, see my *Teaching Transformation: Transcultural Classroom Dialogues.*

4. I borrow the term "queer sociality" from Paola Bacchetta.

Conclusion

Remember Our Past, Exploring Future Possibilities

Phillip A. Boda

From the onset of the colonial project in the Americas, women of color have charged those working toward equity to envision the nature of power and oppression as being more nuanced that singular, myopic views of homogeneity within markers of difference and among them (see Sayer's (1997) translation of 17th-century poet, Sor Juana Inés de la Cruz, for evidence for this claim's derivation). In turn, women such as Frances Ellen Watkins Harper (Harper, 1891) and Anna Julia Cooper (Cooper, 1892/1988; May, 2012) in the late 19th century to Claudia Jones (Jones, 1947) and the Combahee River Collective Statement (Collective, 1979) in the late 20th century have provided substantial Black feminist thought (along with Chicana [Anzaldúa, 1987] and Asian American feminists [Shah, 1997]) that the continual maintenance of the polemic view of oppression through male and/or white views has not shifted in relation to how we take up our critical, collective charge toward equity in education and beyond. Indeed, these are the shoulders we stand on in this volume – critical and rebellious women of color seeking equity for all.

This conclusion, therefore, is for all y'all – to echo Emdin's (2016) title – to start to really think about why you are in education, and what is your charge as a human being living in a society where Race(d)/Trans+/Queer/Female/Disabled bodies are devalued so much that their deaths are justified within colonial-carcel logics of 'perceptions of safety,' in the face of grown adults – supposedly trained in de-escalation strategies – denying these marked bodies of life. This reality demands action, which is why this volume is important for all stakeholders in education, and arguably beyond. I know, for me, teachers throughout my years of schooling have provided that one hopefully glimpse of promise for the future: From the aide that gave me a hug every day in elementary school to my high school teacher taking me to attend mandatory, weekly juvenile justice

P.A. Boda (ed.), Essays on Exclusion, 163–172.

requirements, teachers changed my life, and I dare say that this book charges you to do the same. In turn, I want to end this volume thinking about a (re)narration for self-preservation, to move toward a critical, collective path that recognizes the power of narratives in our schools to persevere toward the goal that these giants have paved for us.

Re-narrating Representation and Self as Praxis

LeRoi Jones (A.K.A. Amiri Baraka) wrote one of his seminal works, *Blues People: Negro Music in White America*, in 1963 and updated the introduction in 1999. In his new introduction, Baraka spoke of the ways that creating this book, and affirming his inner thoughts and yearnings, made him "reach for more and more and more of what I had carried for years, for more of what I had to say, *for more of myself*" (Baraka, 1999, p. vii, italics added). In turn, he elaborated on the importance of rediscovering himself within the contents of the book's creation and the possibilities that it contained when we start to think about how narratives include and exclude:

> That is, how to measure this world in which we find ourselves, where we are not at all happy, but clearly able to understand and hopefully, one day, to transform. How to measure my own learning and experience and to set out a system of evaluation, weights, and meaning. (Baraka, 1999, p. viii).

While Amiri Baraka contextualizes his yearnings within the subject of music, its history, commodification, and social impact related to race and representation/appropriation in America, the nature of his call and articulation of self-exploration hold true throughout this volume, even as the authors position themselves within and among educational spaces. Too true is the reality that when representation shapes and shades myopic and stereotypical narratives for Others, while developing more nuanced roles and perceptions of white America as the 'norm,' we find exclusion operating overtly to the benefit of some and the detriment of others – and, in turn, this creates what Kelly Oliver coins as *The Colonization of the Psychic Space* (2004). This takes form in both a material sense of understanding one's value in an overall society but inevitably leads to more rhetorical and psycho-social implications that are pertinent for understanding and pursuing equity, if we choose to take on that charge.

In alignment with this call for self-rediscovery through inquiry into how socio-cultural contexts, such as the entertainment industry and education, embolden some narratives while neglecting others, bell hooks provides an additional layer to these types of analysis that is pertinent for our critical, collective journey toward equity in education to be fulfilled, specifically in relation to what narratives we teach our children and how it affects them (1994, p. 199, 200, 205). hooks' framing and her (re)narration of Christopher Columbus follows suit with the ways that education scholars have begun to envision the historical structuring of schools as sites where cultural production is not only enforced (Cole, 2005; Oikonomidoy, Salas, Karam, Warren, & Steinmann, 2018), but also sites where teachers play a pivotal role in this process that often relegates education to an assimilationist cultural purpose (Birman & Tran, 2017).

To say that our schools are microcosms of larger societal goals is not only a poignant remark but a necessary recognition if we seek to change the lived realities for students that have been excluded within these contexts. In this same chapter, bell hooks also illuminates the ways in which Columbus positioned the Indigenous peoples of the Americas as 'easily dominated' and, in turn, 'impoverished' in relation to European standards of civility that they did not meet due to their lack of materiality related to 'Europeanness' and, in turn, 'whiteness,' which alluded to his rationale of why these peoples were seen as expendable and collateral damage to the overall goal of ascertaining material wealth by any means necessary. This, then, also challenges us to think about "poverty" and its impact on the narratives we use for ourselves and others in the present day, specifically in relation to education embodying these larger cultural commitments, given that "poverty" differentially subjects some marked as different to more vulnerability than others in relation to structural, representational, and political realities (Crenshaw, 1991).

On "Poverty" and Education: A (Re)Narration

On the next page I have created a chart from U.S. Census data reporting the percentages of people living in poverty within the United States guided by some of the specific positionalities taken up in this volume's chapters for the years 2016 and 2017. What positionalities stand out as the greatest preponderance for the reader over these two years? What does not surprise you? Now, I want you to think about what poverty means for *intersecting* markers of difference from this chart: What about women of color compared to white men (Patrick, 2017) or LGBTQ youth of color (Page, 2017)? Also, what does "poverty" mean in terms of housing stability across race, class, and gender lines (Greenberg, Gershenson & Desmond, 2016), as well as its effect when these intersecting markers of difference determine resource acquisition and efficacy (Greene, 2018)? Indeed, how we envision what equity 'looks like' and whom it is designed to serve most is, unfortunately, disproportionate in negative ways toward these intersecting markers of difference. Over the course of this book, we have looked at different identities and the ways that exclusionary ideologies and practices – our praxes – position them as less-than, as markers of difference that have historically and presently been denied accessible and equitable participation in education that is meaningful and empowering.

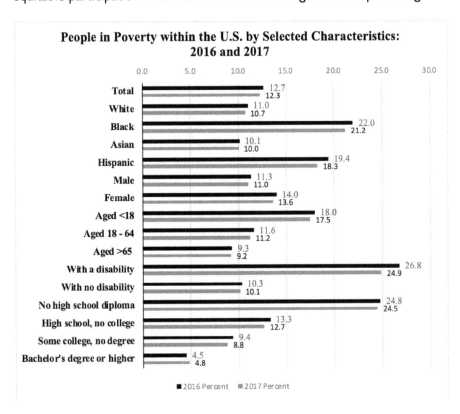

People in Poverty within the U.S. by Selected Characteristics: 2016 and 2017

Data Source: U.S. Census Bureau, Current Population Survey, 2017 and 2018 Annual Social and Economic Supplements. Data retrieved from Table 3 on the following U.S. Census website on February 6th, 2019: https://www.census.gov/data/tables/2018/demo/income-poverty/p60-263.html. Data last updated: September 12th, 2018 by J. Semega, K. Fontenot, and M. Kollar. REPORT NUMBER P60-263

To conclude this volume, I wish to parse out the importance of 'poverty' and its undergirding label that affects all positionalities, in doing so I want the reader to think about the ways in which we can re-think equity being intimately tied to larger goals of alleviating poverty's impact, not in order to claim the banishment of a 'savage' or 'primitive' way of life (as 'poverty' is often represented in mass media and entertainment as detriments to 'civilization' as it currently exists for the privileged in America), but to attack exclusion at one of its basal derivatives. In light of recent arguments about economic status and academic achievement over the past 10 years that have been couched in the representation of the poor as living in a denigrated reality without love, respect, and dignity, we need to challenge our perceptions of how life is narrated by some at the dispense of others, specifically those who have been affected by economic disenfranchisement as part of the neo-colonial process and the onset of modernity as a goal (Mignolo, 2012). We cannot idly suggest that narratives do not affect the lived realities of people in our society, or how outsiders narrate communities not familiar to their own.

In turn, 'poverty' in the burgeoning popular field of neuroscience and education has become a variable seen to negatively affect neurobiological development along the lines of language, executive function, and memory among children subjected to the reality of being 'poor' (cf. Farah, 2017; Hair, Hanson, Wolfe, & Pollak, 2015), arguing that to address the academic achievement, one charge is to address 'poverty' in systematic ways through policy. However, this argument lacks a logic structure that critically addresses the nuanced nature of poverty affecting persons marked as different in American society as being subjected to contextual reality related to economics differently through the lens of using the Great Depression as a case in point beyond myopic statistical analysis (i.e., Golden, 2016). At the same time, scholars have also studied other predictive variables in similar contexts subject to poverty and have found that perceptions that both teachers and students hold about students' capabilities and capacities integral to the process of learning predict academic achievement along similar effect sizes and strengths (Claro, Paunesku, & Dweck, 2016; Dell'Angelo, 2016). This means that the way teachers think about students in terms of their capability to learn, and how students think about themselves as learners, have just as much of an influence as living in 'poverty' in terms of predictive value for specific measures of academic achievement often used in educational research.

These complementary studies shed light on the nature of specific contextual factors as having critical importance to how and in what ways students being subjected to poverty are mediated by the categorical label of 'poor' in the generalized sense. In other words, these scholars have identified and supported through statistical analyses that the label of 'poverty' is insufficient to describe and fully predict whether a student within a particular economic caste will achieve academically. Moreover, these studies also illuminate how the label of poverty can be parsed out in nuanced ways to describe attributes of context as influencing student academic achievement through more specific factors such as early exposure to community violence (Saxbe et al., 2018) and household instability (Garrett-Peters et al., 2016). To understand the label and influence of 'poverty' in the context of wanting student to achieve in academics, then, requires teachers, researchers, and administration – all stakeholders in education, as it were – to deconstruct particular narratives about what poverty is, how it influences their students, and what role these stakeholders play in pursuing inclusion and equity for all students.

Indeed, both of the aforementioned attributes (violence and instability) describe contextual factors that are not distinct to poverty. Rather, these factors emerge from the larger society's sustainment of the poor being positioned within a perception of individual deviancy and defect that prevent them from being upwardly mobile in social structures that would mediate the preponderance of these factors. In agreement with these claims that poverty is more nuanced than a mere label of socioeconomic status (SES), others have also found that gaps in academic achievement among 'poor' youth of color are significantly mediated by students' perception of safety in their schools, and that more positive (and effective) school climates also predict academic achievement within populations such as these (Caughy, Mills, Brinkley, & Owen, 2018; Ruiz, McMahon, & Jason, 2018). Put simply, 'poverty' and its association to 'academic achievement' is not as cut and dry as stating unquestionably that the label 'poor' is a description of monetary capital that, thus, will undoubtedly negatively affect student outcomes. This is a more general cultural description of poverty, but in the context of schooling and students this definition loses credence when thinking about how to work toward ameliorating the achievement gap and paying into the educational debt owed to students who have been disenfranchised from equitable and accessible participation in quality educational experiences (Ladson-Billings, 2006). But what does this mean in the context of this book, and of exclusion?

Principally, as we embark on our critical, collective journey toward equity in education, more often than not we are describing and working with students subjected to what we view as 'impoverished' contexts; however, these contexts, just like the people living within them, have particular experiences – particular narratives about themselves and the world – that shape and shade how teachers and educational stakeholders take up the task of pursing equity in education proposedly with, but often superficially for, them. Thus, to think about exclusion across multiple and intersecting markers of difference, and the contexts that bore, breed, and sustain them – as this book has presented – we must also consider the undergirding rhetoric of poverty influencing our perceptions of difference as being deficit due to its deviation from affluent white, heterosexual, able-bodied, cis-gendered experiences; as being a subject of deficiency, and, instead, consider that the stories we tell ourselves about the 'disenfranchised' are just that – stories. In doing so, we (re)cognize, we start to re-think, the nature of how and in what ways exclusion is produced in these contexts based on *perception* of people rather than the *reality* of their lived experience as being a subject of, and subjected to, exclusion. Kimberlé Crenshaw echoes this request in her seminal work "Mapping the Margins" when she states:

> … [D]elineating difference need not be the power of domination; it can instead be the source of social empowerment and reconstruction … [In turn,] [i]ntersectional subordination need not be intentionally produced; in fact, it is frequently the consequence of the imposition of one burden that intersects with preexisting vulnerabilities to create yet another dimension of disempowerment. (1991, p. 1242, 1249).

This response to the labeling and handling of students subject to subordinated markers of difference is echoed across all of the chapters of this book, each of which contributes pieces to the puzzle of equity in education wherein we are charged to take responsibility for the ways we position ourselves and Others – that our individual beliefs and actions hold power. Throughout the book, we have slated the task of re-approaching equity in education through a challenge of representation – of a challenge to narratives that denigrate people and personhood – and in accordance with this premise we have also begun the task of challenging the stories we tell ourselves about ourselves, as well as those we Other.

Resounding in this call, in this conclusion, we fight for redefining the nature of humanity and our role in this process of creating identities that are valued and disavowed within society, and more specifically in education. In turn, a note from the brilliant theorist Sylvia Wynter helps us on our way to this goal in reconceptualizing human-ness and its derivative forms: "*Being human is a praxis*" (2015, p.23, emphasis in original). Wynter is, in essence, describing what many of the chapters in this book seek to make apparent and visible in terms of narrative, experience, and exclusion: To work toward equity for all, our understandings of what human-ness means needs redefinition in explicit ways that take into consideration both that the body is inherently marked as a political subject due to our individual evaluations of people as similar to or foreign from our own positionality, and also that the construction of those positionalities are not static and immovable but, rather, that they will shift based on context and the parties interacting within that context in ways that describe our humanity as ongoing praxes. That narratives created *in context* matter.

As you have surely read throughout this book, we have delved into the intimate stories and experiences that those subjected to Othering have endured. However, this is not where the reader is being asked to remain stoic as if they do not have a role to play, or power to yield, in contexts such as schools. Rather than lamenting and anguishing over the processes and products of exclusion, the authors in this volume extend an olive branch to those that may have participated in this process of exclusion in the past so that new ways of being a stakeholder in education interested in equity can take hold. By highlighting that being human is a praxis, and that the very nature of our species is centralized around praxis – of understanding our own thoughts and stories, of acting deliberately or subconsciously on those ideas, and of being reflective of actions that exclude – Sylvia Wynter describes how and why narratives, especially those different from your own, are in need of (re)conceptualization, now more than ever. In turn, the argument is such that if we as educators and stakeholders can begin to break down our previously held understandings that embolden a static humanity onto specific identities, while assuming a pluralistic humanity among identities positioned as primary ways of knowing and being, we can enact a critical praxis in schools that value difference as an asset rather than a limitation, or struggle to overcome by any means necessary. That we can move toward equity *by design*.

Moving Forward through Personal Responsibility

Here I leave the reader with merely a reference from Paulo Freire (1998) – the father of Critical Pedagogy – to purposefully not conclude with a specific set of ideals to 'achieve equity' and point the reader toward more nuanced narrations of schooling for their journey toward equity in education to have a path, of sorts. Some may resent this pedagogical move but I hope that it sparks an unsettling of understandings in the reader about how and in what ways our perceptions of, and expectations for, equity may hold for ourselves and others, as well as how we may start to take stock of our own ownership in the processes and products that have led to sustained exclusion of students in our global societies. It is here, in the space between knowing and unknown that liberatory praxis takes hold in the most authentic way – as a personal commitment to understanding ourselves as a set of experiences we use to justify the ways we position Others through exclusionary praxes and goals of assimilation that inherently seek to deny those being subjected to this process from addressing and responding to their own subjective positions (Oliver, 2004), the subjectivity that is created when different positionalities interact, and the contexts that sustain the assumption that some lives matter more than others. I ask the reader to take charge and put in the effort to work toward equity in education – toward an equitable praxis that includes all students – with the goal in mind to not sensationalize experiences as dogma or martyrdom and, instead, view inquiries into narratives as the starting point from which new ways of viewing ourselves and Others takes place. In doing so, we ask ourselves the following questions: What type of teacher am I, and what type of teacher do I want to be remembered for? The answers will guide you forward.

References

Anzaldúa, G. (1987). *Borderlands: la frontera* (Vol. 3). San Francisco: Aunt Lute.

Birman, D., & Tran, N. (2017). When worlds collide: Academic adjustment of Somali Bantu students with limited formal education in a US elementary school. *International Journal of Intercultural Relations, 60*, 132-144.

Caughy, M. O., Mills, B., Brinkley, D., & Owen, M. T. (2018). Behavioral self-regulation, early academic achievement, and the effectiveness of urban schools for low-income ethnic minority children. *American Journal of Community Psychology, 61*, 372-385.

Claro, S., Paunesku, D., & Dweck, C. S. (2016). Growth mindset tempers the effects of poverty on academic achievement. *Proceedings of the National Academy of Sciences, 113*, 8664-8668.

Cole, M. (2005). Cross-cultural and historical perspectives on the developmental consequences of education. *Human Development, 48*, 195-216.

Collective, C. R. (1979). The Combahee river collective: A Black feminist statement. In Z. R. Eisenstein (Ed.), *Capitalist patriarchy and the case for socialist feminism* (pp.362-372). New York, NY: Monthly Review Press.

Cooper, A. J. (1892/1988). *A Voice from the South.* Oxford University Press.

Crenshaw, K. (1991). Mapping the margins: Intersectionality, identity politics, and violence against women of color. *Stanford Law Review,* 1241-1299.

Dell'Angelo, T. (2016). The power of perception: Mediating the impact of poverty on student achievement. *Education and Urban Society, 48*, 245-261.

Emdin, C. (2016). *For White folks who teach in the hood... and the rest of y'all too: Reality pedagogy and urban education.* Beacon Press.

Farah, M. J. (2017). The neuroscience of socioeconomic status: Correlates, causes, and consequences. *Neuron, 96*(1), 56-71.

Freire, P. (1998). *Pedagogy of freedom: Ethics, democracy, and civic courage.* Rowman & Littlefield.

Garrett-Peters, P. T., Mokrova, I., Vernon-Feagans, L., Willoughby, M., Pan, Y., & Family Life Project Key Investigators. (2016). The role of household chaos in understanding relations between early poverty and children's academic achievement. *Early Childhood Research Quarterly, 37*, 16-25.

Golden, A. L. (2016). Association between child poverty and academic achievement. *JAMA pediatrics, 170*, 178-179.

Greenberg, D., Gershenson, C., & Desmond, M. (2016). Discrimination in evictions: Empirical evidence and legal challenges. *Harv. CR-CLL Rev., 51*, 115-158

Greene, J. T. (2018). Categorical exclusions: How racialized gender regulation reproduces reentry hardship. *Social Problems.* Doi: 10.1093/socpro/spy023

Hair, N. L., Hanson, J. L., Wolfe, B. L., & Pollak, S. D. (2015). Association of child poverty, brain development, and academic achievement. *JAMA pediatrics, 169*, 822-829.

Harper, F. E. W. (1891). *Sketches of southern life*. Ferguson Bros. & Company, printers.

Jones, C. (1947). An end to the neglect of the problems of Negro women. *Political Affairs*, Reprinted from June 1949, p. 18.

Ladson-Billings, G. (2006). From the achievement gap to the education debt: Understanding achievement in US schools. *Educational Researcher, 35*(7), 3-12.

May, V. M. (2012). *Anna Julia Cooper, visionary Black feminist: A critical introduction*. Routledge.

McKittrick, K. (Ed.). (2014). *Sylvia Wynter: On being human as praxis*. Duke University Press.

Mignolo, W. D. (2012). *Local histories/global designs: Coloniality, subaltern knowledges, and border thinking*. Princeton University Press.

Oikonomidoy, E., Salas, R. G., Karam, F. J., Warren, A. N., & Steinmann, T. (2018). Locating newcomer students in educational research in the US: a review of the literature from 2000-2017. *Pedagogy, Culture & Society*, 1-20.

Oliver, K. (2004). *The colonization of psychic space: A psychoanalytic social theory of oppression*. U of Minnesota Press.

Page, M. (2017). Forgotten youth: Homeless LGBT youth of color and the Runaway and Homeless Youth Act. *Northwestern Journal of Law & Social Policy, 12*(2), 17-45.

Patrick, K. (2017). National snapshot: Poverty among women & families, 2016. Washington D.C.: National Women's Law Center

Ruiz, L. D., McMahon, S. D., & Jason, L. A. (2018). The role of neighborhood context and school climate in school-level academic achievement. *American Journal of Community Psychology, 61*, 296-309.

Saxbe, D., Khoddam, H., Piero, L. D., Stoycos, S. A., Gimbel, S. I., Margolin, G., & Kaplan, J. T. (2018). Community violence exposure in early adolescence: Longitudinal associations with hippocampal and amygdala volume and resting state connectivity. *Developmental science*, e12686.

Sayers, P. (1997). Sor Juana Inés de la Cruz. Poems, protest, and a dream. New York, NY: Penguin Classics.

Shah, S. (Ed.) (1997). *Dragon ladies: Asian American feminists breathe fire*. South End Press.

About the Authors

Phillip A. Boda, Ph.D., received his doctorate from Teachers College, Columbia University in Science Education. Afterwards held his first Post-Doctoral Researcher position at Stanford University from 2017-2019 and starts his second Post-doctoral appointment in 2019 at the University of California – Berkeley. His work encompasses urban teacher education, cultural/disability studies in STEM education, and the use of novel educational technologies.

Felicia Moore Mensah, Ph.D., is Professor of Science Education at Teachers College, Columbia University. Her research addresses issues of diversity and equity in science teacher education. Recent research utilizes critical race theory and intersectionality to transform teacher education research and practice.

Carlos Adams, Ph.D., received his graduate degree from Washington State University in American Studies. He currently teaches American Minority and Ethnic Studies as an adjunct instructor at Green River College in Washington State. His work explores concepts of hope, machismo, and the development of new and creative futures to decolonize the mind and body.

Yolanda Sealey-Ruiz, Ph.D., is an Associate Professor of English Education at Teachers College, Columbia University (TC). She is the founder of the Racial Literacy Project at TC. Her research includes racial literacy development, equity pedagogy, and culturally responsive teaching.

Shamari Reid is a doctoral candidate in the department of curriculum and teaching at Teachers College, Columbia University. Currently, he is engaged in his dissertation work which explores the agency of Black LGBTQ+ youth in New York City.

Cathryn Devereaux is a doctoral student in the Department of Curriculum and Teaching at Teachers College, Columbia University. Her research interests include participatory studies highlighting the diverse experiences of Black women and girls in urban communities.

Emily A. Nusbaum, Ph.D., is an Assistant Professor in the school of education at University of San Francisco. Her teaching and research position disability studies in education as a transformative alternative to traditional, special education. Emily was named the 2017 Ellen Brantlinger Emerging Scholar Award at the annual DSE Second City Conference.

Danielle Cowley, Ph.D., is an Associate Professor at the University of Northern Iowa. She teaches courses on inclusion, transition, and humanistic behavior supports. Her research focuses on the intersections of gender and disability, inclusive school reform, and culturally sustaining transition practices.

David I. Hernández-Saca, Ph.D., is Assistant Professor of Disability Studies in Education at the Department of Special Education at the University of Northern Iowa.

Amy Petersen, Ed.D., is a Professor at the University of Northern Iowa. She prepares teachers to educate students with significant disabilities and teaches graduate coursework in qualitative research, inclusion, and disability studies in education. Her research interests focus on qualitative methodology, inclusive reform, and intersectional understandings of disability.

Phil Smith, Ph.D., is an educator, and Mad. His most recent book is Writhing Writing: Moving Towards a Mad Poetics (2018). A poet, storyteller, and photographer, he served as President of the Society of Disability Studies.

Shameka N. Powell, Ph.D., is an Assistant Professor of Educational Studies at Tufts University. They combine qualitative research approaches with critical race theory, critical policy frameworks, and queer of color theories to explore educational inequality.

Debbie Sonu, Ph.D., is an Associate Professor of Education at Hunter College and doctoral faculty at The Graduate Center, CUNY. Her scholarly interests include curriculum theory, politically-oriented teaching, and critical childhood studies.

ReAnna S. Roby, Ph.D., currently works as a Researcher at Vanderbilt is a Postdoctoral Researcher at Michigan State University. As a Critical Race Curriculum theorist, Roby's scholarship explores how the narratives of

Black women and girls in science could be used to reconceptualize science curriculum.

Angela Calabrese Barton, Ph.D., is a Professor in the School of Education at the University of Michigan. Working within the intersection of formal/informal education, Calabrese Barton studies the design of teaching-learning environments and experiences that promote expansive learning outcomes, such as critical agency, identity work, and social transformation.

AnaLouise Keating, Ph.D., is a Professor of multicultural women's & gender studies at Texas Woman's University, explores transformation studies, pedagogies, Anzaldúan theories, and womanist spiritual activism. Her most recent book is Transformation Now! Toward a Post-Oppositional Politics of Change.